Higher Education

Patterns of Change in the 1970s

Contributors

W. H. G. Armytage
Professor of Education, University of Sheffield

Stanley Hewett
General Secretary of the Association of Teachers in Colleges and Departments of Education

Patrick Nuttgens
Director of the Leeds Polytechnic

Arnold Kettle
Professor of Literature at the Open University

A. B. Pippard
Cavendish Professor of Physics at Cambridge University

H. A. Jones
Vaughan Professor of Education at Leicester University

W. A. C. Stewart
Vice-Chancellor of the University of Keele

William Walsh
Professor of Commonwealth Literature and Douglas Grant Fellow at the University of Leeds

F. J. Orton
Academic Secretary, University of Sheffield

John Lawlor
(the editor of the symposium)
Professor of English, University of Keele

Higher Education
Patterns of Change in the 1970s

Edited by
John Lawlor

Routledge & Kegan Paul
London and Boston

First published 1972
by Routledge & Kegan Paul Ltd
Broadway House, 68–74 Carter Lane,
London EC4V 5EL and
9 Park Street,
Boston, Mass. 02108, U.S.A.
Printed in Great Britain by
Unwin Brothers Limited
The Gresham Press, Old Woking, Surrey, England
A member of the Staples Printing Group

ISBN 0 7100 7352 6

Contents

Preface

The focus of the present collection is on the changing pattern of tertiary education in one country, the United Kingdom.

Each contributor has had an entirely free hand. I think it will be seen that there is a common stress upon challenges and opportunities rather than problems and difficulties, and a general willingness to re-examine what may hitherto have been too readily assumed.

Like its predecessor, *The New University*, the present collection is offered as a contribution to the widest discussion—in particular, the definition of aims and capabilities in a partnership that must extend right across the board of 'higher education' if it is to meet current and impending needs.

University of Keele,
Staffordshire   JOHN LAWLOR

In lieu of Delphi: what?

W. H. G. Armytage

Professor of Education, University of Sheffield

On 17 July 1961 the National Union of Students presented a memorandum to the Robbins Committee which was described by Lord Robbins as 'excellent . . . well-reasoned and sensible . . . that traversed in an illuminating way' most of the subjects that concerned his committee. Para. 33 reads:[1]

> Another possibility is the establishment of a two-year course of broad further education through which all students wishing to enter higher education must pass. This would be taken in existing institutions of higher education to gain the benefits of participation in a full academic community. Its object would be to give a broad basis of knowledge and some understanding of the inter-relationships of disciplines combined with a certain degree of specialization. On this general foundation the student could proceed to build his specialization without the detrimental effects experienced at present. It would also help to avoid premature selection by giving the student time to feel his way into his chosen subject while testing his choice against a wide range of studies. It is to be presumed that most students would proceed to their special subject in the institutions where they took this general course, although some would wish to change their course and should be able to transfer to other institutions or faculties. The two-year course would be completed with an examination of national standard and would permit those who did not wish to pursue specialist studies to obtain a diploma or certificate in general studies.

Eleven years later, a Committee of Inquiry under Lord James endorsed a similar suggestion in these words:[2]

> It is one of the curiosities of higher education in this country that for the 18-year-old school leaver who does not want to enter employment immediately there is virtually no alternative, apart from certain kinds of training that are specifically vocational, to a 3-year course leading either to a degree or to a teaching qualification. . . . It has been suggested that such a qualification [i.e. the two-year diploma] would be welcomed not only by business, industry and the public service but also by the schools. The schools may see it, for many of their sixth formers who require higher education, as a welcome

alternative to the present university courses which are not necessarily well-suited to the aptitudes and aspirations of all those who are formally qualified to take them. It would be naïve to disregard completely the weight of responsible university opinion questioning whether there is sufficient motivation for university courses, as at present conceived, on the part of many of the formally qualified students who choose to follow them.

The NUS was one of 115 persons and institutions that gave evidence to Robbins. The James proposal was the distillate of the evidence of 587 persons and institutions.

When in search of opinion Sir Francis Galton used to circulate questionnaires 'to people likely to provide trustworthy answers to a string of rather curious and unusual questions'. These he found amongst what he vaguely termed 'educational establishments in Britain and America' as well as Fellows of the Royal Society, members of the French Institute and similarly selective institutions. A more strenuous operation with multiple refinements has been employed in the prospicient exercises in the United States of America. Known as Delphi, it consists of a highly sophisticated battery of reiterated questionnaires[3] designed to obtain a forecast. Delphi was also employed in the United Kingdom with further modifications by the Office of Health Economics.[4] It is a very great pity that it has not yet been employed, to my knowledge, to obtain a forecast of the shape of higher education in Britain in the 1980s.

So intricate and tangled have all questions in modern life become that just after the Second World War Sir Cyril Burt broadcast a suggestion that 'pooling the experiences and opinions of intelligent individuals from every walk of life might often lead to far more trustworthy conclusions on the wider issues . . . than we could possibly hope to extract from the mere specialist or the expert'. Similar sentiments, sharpened by more pressing needs, led to the devising of what might almost be called a 'social technology' of canvassing opinion from those whose natural excellence of mind and character made them understandably reluctant to proffer it at the slightest pretext or at any price. 'The Cambridge pledge' of Mr Edward Short that the Labour Party will fight for a million student places by 1981 demands we consider it.

I

Nothing seems to stay those simple believers in linear extrapolation in education who would laugh to scorn their counterparts in other fields who, using similar apodictic arithmetic, would prophesy that manned spacecraft will be able to accelerate at the speed of light by 1990, or who could regard with confidence the equally suppositious prophecy that immortality will be on the way by the twenty-first century, or that humanity will be enlarging in all directions at the speed of light by A.D. 3990.

Extrapolations of numbers of students seem to have a similar hypnotic effect. It is supposed by some that it will afford an excuse for telescoping all institutions in the higher education sector together into a regional communiversity, and by others that it will still further extend the pecking order of such institutions: making as it were more divisions, as in professional football, where highly active forecasting seems to have developed.

A Delphi might well elicit more responsible forecasts from those other than the saps (a legitimate acronym for self-appointed pontificators who regularly make noises on such matters) whose postures and stances are themselves so predictable that debate is stifled before it begins. For Delphi can elicit other unsuspected limiting factors, even from more reluctant and perhaps more reliable forecasters.

Unless contingency forecasts are available for debate, no proper decisions can be made. Proper decisions are resolutions between carefully explored alternatives. Exploring alternatives has itself become very sophisticated. Mathematical models (built by extrapolation into the future of past time series through correlation analysis) and matrix techniques (to study cross impacts) need supplementing by a searching of expert opinions. Hence (once again) Delphi. Only by supplementing the homework being done on the shape of higher education in the seventies, by a Delphi (as distinct from another conference), would it seem possible to enlist the silent members of the academic community who are naturally chary of airing their views in public.

If such an exercise did no more than involve these otherwise silent members of our community, it would serve a purpose. For encouraged by its anonymity, they would express opinion without being victimized by the labelling process all too common in such discourse. It would be only logical too, that having adopted and adapted costing customs like the Programming, Planning and Budgeting Technique, and given a favourable reception to cost-benefit and cost-analysis techniques, we should indulge ourselves in an exercise which itself sprang from the need to weave guide lines from a flocculence of ideas.

II

Yet though we have had no Delphi scenario, we ourselves were presented with some thirteen propositions that might have well provided the raw material for one. They were posed as questions to the Vice-Chancellors' and Principals' Committee by Mrs Shirley Williams, when Secretary of State. The Vice-Chancellors then referred them to their individual senates, which savaged them. How much better would it have been to have avoided the consensus process by means of a Delphi? We can only guess; for now we shall never know, as stances, once adopted, are not easily relaxed.

The first four of her suggestions seemed to be like ranging shots in an artillery barrage, to bracket rather than hit the target:

(i) a reduction or removal of student grant-aid, coupled with a system of loans; (ii) a similar policy at the postgraduate level; (iii) a more restrictive policy as regards the admission of overseas students; (iv) the requirement that grant-aided students should enter specified kinds of employment for a period after graduation, which might have the effect of reducing applications.

The next four suggestions concern high strategy and deserve most careful study:

(v) the greater use of part-time and correspondence courses as alternatives to full-time courses; (vi) the possibility that the most able should have the opportunity to complete a degree course in two years; (vii) the possibility of some students not proceeding to the customary three-year course, but to a different course lasting only two years and leading to a different qualification; (viii) the possible insertion of a period between school and university which would give school-leavers a better opportunity to formulate their views as to whether or not they wished to proceed to some form of higher education.

The last five suggestions are already on the agenda of many universities' committees, and have been for some time:

(ix) the more extensive use of buildings and equipment including the possibility of reorganization of the academic year; (x) more sharing of facilities between adjacent institutions; (xi) more home-based students; (xii) the development of student housing associations, and other forms of loan-financed provision for student residence; (xiii) some further increase in student/staff ratios.

III

Since these questions were presented, the academic mills have ground out so many scientists and engineers that their employment is becoming a social problem. More than half the annual output of engineers now qualify through CNAA or through the professional institutions. The yield on training as a scientist has drastically declined, so the questions will not have to be answered solely from the point of view of the national need for scientists and technologists. Here one must salute the prospicience of Gannicott and Blaug who cogently prophesied there would be a surplus of scientists. And there is. They quoted an OECD survey showing the UK as training 40 per cent more technologists in relation to the size of the age group than the USA and a higher proportion of pure scientists than any OECD country but the USA.[5] They demolished the arguments of the so-called science lobby as represented by the Committee on Manpower Resources for Science and Technology, and challenged the four assumptions of that committee, namely: (i) the long term shortage of scientists and technologists; (ii) the tendency of the universities to divert the best talent in these fields from industry and the schools; (iii) the flight of such talent from Britain; and (iv) a recognizable, growing swing away from science amongst those at present in the schools who might replace them.

Yet one assumption, far from being demolished, seems to stand out all the more, simply because it was *not* incorporated into the general efflorescence of reports that marked the late sixties, but was printed as an appendix in one of them. This is the suggestion of a two-year degree course. It reappeared as proposition (vi) in the Shirley Williams list. Her proposition (vii) (which suggests a two-year non-degree course for the not so able) was tactically revealed in an inspired whisper from behind the curtain when Lord James decided to test opinion among those involved in the training of teachers. It had an enormous appeal at a time of escalating costs, but it also has academic appeal, since it could well involve a more equitable system generalized tertiary education.

The Swann Committee found the suggestion of a two-year degree course 'stimulating and provocative' but did not endorse it because they thought it 'would require too much of an upheaval in our accustomed habits to be readily acceptable'.[6] As there outlined it was that 'the Bachelor's Degree would be awarded at the end of the period of general education, after two years at the university, so that those who had no wish to pursue specialist studies or receive vocational training could leave at this stage without any sense of failure.' The author of the proposal expressed the hope 'that many students would indeed take this opportunity, for the present inflexible system (including the virtual guarantee of three years to every student) is harmful in setting before too large a proportion of the population the somewhat arbitrary goals which were originally designed for an academic elite.'[7]

Its author, Professor Pippard, considers that 'the present habit of conducting third year honours course in all the principal branches of learning at all universities makes for very inefficient use of the teachers' time, and in many cases does not provide the individual good student with companions of comparable mettle to help develop his powers.' But what makes Professor Pippard's suggestion more uniquely relevant is that without precluding general courses based on Arts and Social Sciences he also envisages a new general science course attracting 'a large number of these uncommitted students who nowadays have no place in scientific dpeartments and must find their education in other fields'. The Pippard proposal (which he offers not as a cut and dried solution but simply as a starting point of debate) is that students graduating with a Bachelor's degree could, after a two-year generalist course, choose between a number of options. They could migrate for an intensive specialized two-year course in conventional fields or they could switch to one- or two-year courses in engineering and other technical sciences, or to schools of education, business, medicine, law, or theology. The diploma would be the appropriate third year award, the Master's degree the appropriate fourth year award. Only after the Master's degree would research proper begin. Thus transfers and switching at the end of the second (or indeed the end of the fourth) year involve switching institutions.

IV

The 'new men' of yesterday are the know-how men of today. Not the highly specialized science graduates of *The Search* but those whom another working party of the Council on Scientific Policy discovered in the United States: the science-based generalist. They can be seen working in the rehearsal centre of most of our problems: the United States of America. In their industries and schools they prefer to recruit such generalists, and not specialists of the type developed by undergraduate courses in the UK.[8] With Ph.D.s in science and engineering a drug on the job market today this is even truer.

In England at most only 40 per cent of the total employment of scientists and technologists could in 1967 be described as being in high level specialist occupations. Hence the Swann Report indicated that 'the main requirement in the future will be for science-based generalists in occupations such as school teaching, general management and administration.' It forecast that 'the total demand in the next few years for research specialists outside industry could well be less than half the numbers expected to qualify in research training with a Ph.D. degree.'[9] How right they have been in the outcome.

Hence their endorsement of a generalist-based first degree on which specialisms could be later built. Though it presented a major problem of adaptation, the Swann Committee hoped to see experiments in every university whereby students of science, technology and engineering could all start from a common first base, equipped with 'some broad understanding of the society in which they will work'. Also, as 'timely for major development in this quinquennium',[10] the Swann Committee suggested the involvement of employers in 'post-experience courses'.

B

V

The Pippard plan (if one may so call it) also deserves discussion in the light of evidence collected by the Willey Report. In this, the NUS (which with 350,000 members is the sixth biggest 'union' in the country) is reported as feeling that 'the curriculum was out of date and did not respond to the need to innovate, improvise [and] solve problems with no precedent'. That students themselves should have considered 'the insufficiency of the academic study' as contributing to student unrest is one interesting item of feedback. Another was that Arts students at Cambridge were questioning 'content as much as, if not more than, the way [their subject] is being taught'. 'A lot of these people', reported the Willey Committee, 'say that what they are being taught in English, History and Economics is irrelevant.'[11]

Taken at the height of the 'student troubles' the Willey Committee's evidence is only one example of the growing practice of eliciting the constructive expression and consideration of student views. But such staff-student committees whether at departmental, faculty or senate level need homework exercises on syllabuses, methods of assessing students' performance, teaching methods, unit courses, and so forth, much of which is properly done at the institutional level. NUS too might run a Delphi of their members in order to establish what students really think about such practical matters as two-year degrees, unit courses, and so forth.

Since the Willey Report, not only has the balance of power in universities, polytechnics and colleges of education been under responsible scrutiny, but so have interrelationships between these institutions themselves. Common lodgings bureaux, health services and common regulations, are ironically not as common as the common membership of Officer Training Corps.

So much indeed did the Willey Committee have in mind the need to co-ordinate the three main components of the higher educational system, that it proposed that a Higher Education Commission, endowed with responsibilities extending to all institutions of higher education, should be established as a national forum and an advisory body to governments as to the needs of the various institutions. This Higher Education Commission was also to include representatives of the local authorities.[12]

Ironically, not one of its fifty-eight recommendations defended the need for a Delphi, which could have trawled in less perturbed waters, and perhaps got better fish.

VI

Now one of the great merits of the two-year degree course is that it envisages students, at the end of their two-year degree course, proceeding not only to universities, but to the polytechnics and colleges of education as well. Of the first, Pippard adds: 'if their educational programmes were combined with major research projects closely associated with industry, these institutions would fulfil a natural role as centres of excellence in the useful arts.'

One could extend this concept by referring to the mobility between universities and government research establishments earlier recommended by the Robbins Committee,[13] or to the report of the Mott Committee. The latter was appointed by the Electronics Research Council of the Ministry of Aviation, and recommended in 1966 that this Ministry's establishments should 'assume a major responsibility for training in this field, and for seeing that the educational potential resulting from its own work is properly utilized'. It also recommended that the research establishments of the Ministry of Aviation should have a threefold mandate for teaching: sandwich courses (which they already had); postgraduate training in technology; and occasional teaching in postgraduate courses. To increase this it suggested that university and technical college staff should, amongst other things, be encouraged to make use of research facilities in establishments and join in establishment programmes. Mott also suggested that the location of neighbouring research establishments should be taken into account when siting new universities and colleges.[14]

Now the Mott thesis, if I may call it so, that new universities or colleges should be sited in areas where the facilities of neighbouring research establishments can be utilized, indirectly raises yet again the familiar problem of university development: that of centres of special excellence. For this would seem to suppose that such a new university—centred upon nuclear physics, say—would at a bound become a centre of special excellence in that field. It would be fatuous to suppose otherwise. But are there not counterparts for training recruits to the Social Services of the post-Seebohm world?

That study and research are becoming (and will become even more) affiliated to research establishments in industry or in government indicates that we are moving on lines originally laid down in the USSR rather than the USA. Here significant noises have been made by Mr Aubrey Jones. For as early as 10 July 1961 in the House of Commons he hammered home the theme that not only had we to treat science and technology more seriously but he added 'it is inevitable that we treat it on something approaching Soviet terms . . . we have to go some way in adopting the planning methods of the Soviet Union in science and technology'.[15]

This increasing co-operation between research institutions, universities and polytechnics is reflected in the attempts now being made to find a substitute for the word 'university'. So far, these neologisms have been singularly unhappy. 'Multiversity', 'quniversity', 'polyversity' (cynics have suggested 'subversity' or 'perversity') indicate that its relationships with other institutions in the tertiary sector are becoming more important. Terms like 'comprehensive university',[16] 'quniversity',[17] and 'polyversity'[18] are really attempts to describe the process of colligation, or agglutination, now taking place in higher education. This process has been described by *Nature*, a journal which a hundred years ago was campaigning for a Minister of Science. Four years ago it editorialized:[19]

When asked, academics will now admit that Britain probably does not need the 46 universities which now exist, particularly when the balkanization of London University still further fragments the system. Many institutions are numerically too small to sustain the range of activities expected of a university —they would make quite respectable liberal arts colleges but cannot hope, as most of them do, to support vigorous graduate programmes as well as a full range of undergraduate courses. This is not merely dispiriting for people who teach at these universities but often—not always—needlessly cramping for the students and a source of inefficiency as well. The UGC has for some time been trying to encourage a concentration of resources within the universities and can boast (as it does in its latest report) of having persuaded three schools of agriculture to go out of existence. But this is a very small beginning and, although the schemes for collaboration which numbers of universities have set up for themselves seem to promise well, they too are only scratching the surface of the problem. In short, if the universities are not to amalgamate with polytechnics, then should not some of them seriously consider amalgamating with each other? And should not the Government encourage a tendency in this direction by giving an assurance that universities which take such drastic steps (for them) will afterwards be able to enjoy the benefits of size?

Note the phrase 'if the universities are not to amalgamate with polytechnics'. *Nature* asked 'might it not have been a better course to have begun by working out means by which polytechnics and universities could share facilities and teachers and even, on some occasions, the same boards of governors and Privy Council Charters? And is it even now too late?' By January 1970 Mr Jack Straw was calling for 'polyversities'—debalkanized higher education units comprising not only the local universities and the polytechnics but the colleges of education too.

Such debalkanization looked like emerging at the undergraduate level before the James Report, when the colleges of education were experimenting with the B.Ed. My own university for instance now has a faculty of Education and Information Studies on which sit representatives of the colleges of education elected by their own academic boards. The sandwich principle was beginning in universities other than the former CATs. This could be seen in the postgraduate courses like those in semi-conductor technology run jointly by the University of Southampton and the Conference of the Electronics Industry, or that in microelectronics and the engineering of electronic devices run by the Universities in Edinburgh and by Imperial College. Though financially supported by the UGC these owe much to CNAA.[20] Here one should acknowledge the vital contribution of the present director of the Newcastle Polytechnic, G. S. Bosworth, whose report on *Education and training requirements for the electrical and mechanical manufacturing industries* published in 1966 established the concept of a 'matching course' to ease the transition from the academic to the industrial world.

Yet another CNAA precedent was commended to universities by the Sutherland Committee which examined the relation between universities and the Government Research Establishments. This hoped to see 'further progress' in the teaching of university courses or the supervision of universities by industrial as well as college staff.[21]

VII

Polyvalence seems the only principle which would make sense to intending entrants. Interpreting what is offered to them on rational grounds is increasingly difficult; hence the rise of 'consultant agencies'. A Delphi of former students at colleges of education might well find that the colleges were so good in the field of human relations that some of them too should be considered as centres of excellence in the various areas round the country, as the polytechnics would be in any Pippardian model of tomorrow. A Delphi might well have depolarized the field of forces operating for and against James, by presenting a forward view decontaminated of the 'collapsive process' of committees. It might also provide far better information for decision-making in institutions themselves. Indicators of our graduate population 'going sour on society' intensify the need for supplementing the ever more intricate consultative techniques adopted within and without institutions, and offset the tyranny of the professions in the instant functional parliaments created by any official enquiry.

Though it used to be said that we have the best written and least read blue books in the world, the verbal ambiguities of the statement would raise, from those who read them, a smile as tired as those whose names are affixed to them must surely be. And without diminishing in any way the value of Swann, McCarthy, Sutherland, Mott and James, Rothschild and Dainton (the ever-unrolling calendar of sociographers makes even this list out-of-date as soon as it is compiled) one might ask (as a future historian surely would) why in an age of social invention did a system so involved in the future not at least try out a technique for descrying its unfolding contours? Much as one reveres the modern oracles, some of the near-ribald techniques of 'consultation' might well be replaced. The 'continuing dialogue'[22] called for by Rothschild between the customer, the Chief Scientist, the Controller R and

D, and those concerned with the actual prosecution of R and D assumes that the therapy of discussion is needed by those who want to get on with their jobs. Similar assumptions underlie the bumbling consultative processes of academic decision-making, which now engage too many people's minds too long for too little purpose.

If some group tries, they might consider the alternative processes for providing full-time higher education for Mr Short's million in the 1980s. Those who cannot accept the linear expansion of what is would like to know what might be.

What might be is what Lord James himself called 'a radical new approach' in which 'experiment with unit courses' would give 'maximum freedom of choice to students'.[23] One cannot help thinking that James has presented an eyeball to eyeball confrontation with the universities knowing that the university eye is half closed.

Notes

1 *Higher Education Evidence—Part One Volume A. Written and Oral Evidence received by the Committee appointed by the Prime Minister under the Chairmanship of Lord Robbins*, London, HMSO, 1963, Cmnd 2154—VI, pp. 221–2, 237.

2 *Teacher Education and Training.* A Report by a Committee of Inquiry appointed by the Secretary of State for Education and Science, under the Chairmanship of Lord James of Rusholme, HMSO, 1972, p. 46.

3 Olaf Helmer Hirschberg, *The Use of the Delphi Technique in Problems of Educational Innovations*, Santa Monica: Rand Corportion, 1966. For a recent Delphi see T. J. Gordon and R. E. Le Bleu, 'Employee benefits, 1970–1985', *Harvard Business Review*, Jan.–Feb. 1970, pp. 93–107. For those to whom the Delphi method is new the following are useful: Olaf Helmer, *The Delphi Method for systematizing judgements about the future* UCLA, 1966;Olaf Helmer *Social Technology*, Basic Books, 1966; E. Jantsch, *Technological Forecasting in Perspective*, OECD, 1967; Juri Pill, 'The Delphi Method: substance ,context, a critique and an annotated bibliography', *Socio-Econ. Plan. Sci.*, 1971.

4 *Medicines in the 1990s, a technological forecast*, London: Office of Health Economics, 1969.

5 K. G. Gannicott and Mark Blaug, 'Manpower forecasting since Robbins: a Science lobby in action', *Higher Education Review*, Vol. 2, No. 1, 1969, pp. 68, 72.

6 Professor Pippard's proposals are contained in Appendix E of the Committee on Manpower Resources for Science and Technology: *The Flow into Employment of Scientists, Engineers and Technologists. Report of the Working Group on Manpower for Scientific Growth*, London: HMSO, 1968, Cmnd 3760 (the Swann Report), pp. 106–10, p. 78.

7 *Ibid.*, pp. 106–10.

8 *The Employment of Highly Specialised Graduates: a comparative study in the U.K. and the U.S.A.*, Science Policy Studies, No. 3, London: HMSO

9 Swann Report, p. 74.

10 *Op. cit.*, p. 80.

11 *Report from the Select Committee on Education and Science: Student Relations*, Vol. 1, London: HMSO, 1969, 449–i, paras 366 and 373, pp. 85, 87.

12 *Report of the Committee on Local Authority and Allied Personal Social Services*, London: HMSO, 1968, Cmnd 3703.

13 Cmnd 2154, 1963, Recommendation 63.

14 *The Educational Role of the Ministry of Aviation Establishments*, London: HMSO, 1966, Code No. 56–66.

15 *Hansard*, 10 July 1961, p. 82.

16 Robert Cuddihay, Douglas Gowan and Colin Lursey, *The Red Paper*, Edinburgh: Islander Publications, 1970.

17 John Vaizey, 'People's Universities', *Nature*, Vol. 220, 30 November 1968, pp. 859–60.

18 Jack Straw at the NUS conference January 1970.

19 *Nature*, Vol. 220, 30 November 1968.

20 *Report of the Flow of Candidates in Science and Technology into Higher Education*, London: HMSO, Cmnd 3541, 1968.

21 *Report of the Working Party on Liaison between Universities and Government Research Establishments*, London: HMSO, Cmnd 3222 (the Sutherland Report).

22 *A Framework for Governmental Research and Development*, London: HMSO, Cmnd 4814, 1971, p. 9.

23 *Teacher Education and Training*, para. 4.22.

The futures of the colleges of education

Stanley Hewett

*General Secretary of the Association of Teachers
in Colleges and Departments of Education*

The inquiry conducted by the James Committee and, more importantly, the ways in which all concerned respond to the possibilities it outlines will have decisive consequences for the development of higher education in this country. The Committee has not exceeded its terms of reference:[1] it was inevitable that considering the future of a major sector of higher education would have implications for the future pattern of the total higher education jig-saw. Whether the Committee as constituted was an appropriate body to be so decisively involved in such a matter and whether they had adequate time and resources for the job, is now an academic matter. They have been so involved and the task now is to see how the possibilities presented may be best utilized.

I

How the colleges came, at this particular point in time, to be such a crucially important factor in the development of higher education and why they crystallize so many of the political issues involved in that development deserves some consideration. The colleges have been prisoners of their history and tradition:[2] at the end of the sixties it had become obvious that the tensions created by the conflict between their past role and their present situation was in need of urgent resolution. A number of major issues came to the crunch at the same time and their common meeting ground was the James Committee.

Until the 1944 Education Act there were two maintained systems of education in England and Wales—elementary and secondary—with the possibility of transferring from the first to second by virtue of brains or money, preferably both. Each system had broadly speaking its own source of teacher supply. The secondary schools with their subject-centred tradition recruited mainly graduates whose degrees were regarded as qualifications of professional competence, though a proportion of recruits voluntarily sought post-graduate professional training. The elementary schools recruited, in the main, certificated teachers from the training colleges where the emphasis was on training rather than on personal education. The colleges in which this process took place were restricted and restrictive institutions, closely controlled by the providing bodies, both voluntary and local authority, which had founded them in order to secure an adequate supply of the kind of teachers they wanted for their schools. They contrasted in almost every conceivable way with the autonomous and prestigious universities with their tradition of learning in an atmosphere of free inquiry.

These two routes into teaching divided the profession into first- and second-class members, the status depending not on professional competence but on the qualifications held and the place where they were obtained. The differential salaries and career prospects of the two classes inside the profession reinforced the original distinctions in no uncertain terms. The history of teacher education has been the story of successive attempts by the colleges and the teachers to unify the profession by abolishing the distinctions, and steady resistance to such attempts by central and local government, neither of which looks with any great favour on a more expensive profession, educated in institutions over which they cannot exercise direct control. The administrators prefer to regard the colleges as extensions of the school system they were created to serve.

Even before the McNair Report (1944)[3] some progress had been made in eroding the distinction. A few London colleges entered some of their students for external London degrees which they took concurrently with their professional studies leading to the Teacher's Certificate. One college, Westminster, developed special arrangements with certain colleges of London University at which Westminster students could undertake full-time under-graduate study and follow their graduation with professional training at the College. The Board of Education was at best lukewarm towards these ambitious variations in the general pattern of college work and there was no encouragement for its extension. The Westminster model did not survive the removal of the college to Oxford in 1959.

II

The two traditions of teacher education began to come closer together after the *annus mirabilis* of English education—1944. The Education Act of that year abolished the elementary schools and the restricted secondary schools and substituted primary and secondary stages of education through which all pupils would pass. (In its tripartite division of secondary education it also began the irresistible move towards comprehensive secondary education.) The McNair Report in the same year recommended *inter alia* that the colleges should not only train but also concurrently educate their students, thus clearly recognizing that the colleges had a higher education function to perform. To emphasize the point it further recommended that the college course should be of three years' duration. With the notable exception of Cambridge all universities involved eventually set up Institutes or Schools of Education with colleges as constituent members, and these university bodies, by awarding the Teacher's Certificate, became responsible for underwriting the standards of entrants to the teaching profession. The acute post-war shortage of teachers and the consequent necessity to maintain the highest output from the colleges held the course at two years. First- and second-class membership of the profession still existed although the restructured school system made such distinctions anachronistic and hence more invidious. The first- and second-class members worked alongside each other in the secondary stage of education and were expected, along with parents and pupils, to believe in 'parity of esteem'. The growth of comprehensive secondary education exacerbated the tensions to an intolerable degree.

Throughout the fifties, pressure to establish a three-year course mounted and was materially assisted by a happy miscalculation on the part of the National Advisory Council for the Training and Supply of Teachers which led the Council to a belief that in the sixties teacher supply if maintained at the existing rate would outstrip demand. Rather than reduce the number of places in the colleges the Council recommended that numbers should be maintained but output reduced by the introduction of the three-year course in 1960.[4] This was accepted by the government of the day which was informed almost immediately afterwards by the NACTST[5] that for a variety of reasons there would in fact be an acute shortage of teachers throughout the decade. To its undying credit the government stood by its commitment to the three-year course.

The Robbins Committee[6] in its inquiry into the provision of higher education included the colleges. Before the first three-year course was complete they had decided to recommend that college students with the requisite ability should be allowed to take a four-year course and receive the degree of Bachelor of Education from the universities which provided the Institutes of Education of which their colleges were constituent members. This was accepted by the government though the recommendation to incorporate the colleges fully into the universities via Schools of Education was not.

The combined effect of these three virtually simultaneous phenomena—the acute shortage of teachers, the introduction of a three-year course, and the institution of a four-year course for some—was a massive expansion of the numbers of students in training and fundamental changes in the nature of the colleges and the work they undertook. A later development, the requirement that all graduates wishing to teach in maintained schools should have a professional qualification, added impetus to the movement already in train by vastly increasing the number of post-graduates in the colleges.

In 1956 there were 26,000 students in the colleges (13,000 annual intake). In 1971 there were 110,000 students (39,000 annual intake): 2,872 B.Ed. degrees were awarded and 39·1 per cent of these were first- or second-class honours degrees.[7] Acceptance for post-graduate courses in 1971 showed 4,037 in the colleges and 5,077 in university education departments.[8] The gap between college educated/trained teachers and university educated/trained teachers had narrowed to such an extent that it was increasingly difficult to justify the existence of a gap at all. The pressure for its abolition by fully integrating the colleges into the system of higher education had never been stronger or more justified. Supported by forecasts that the percentage of the relevant age group obtaining 2 'A' levels would rise to 24·2 per cent by 1980/1, the colleges could reasonably ask Lord James that their entrance requirements should be raised to the minimum demanded of university entrants and that students thus qualified on entrance should proceed to degree awards.[9] The academic/educational aspirations of the colleges had clearly reached a crisis point.

The ultra-rapid increase in the number of students training to be teachers resulted in the odd situation that the number of intending teachers on pre-service courses of professional training was, in 1971, roughly one-third of the number of teachers actually in service. This ratio obviously could not be allowed to continue once the shortage of teachers had been made good. The tapering off of college output when linked to the increasing numbers of graduates coming forward for training necessitated a planned and fairly sharp reduction in the intake of intending teachers to the colleges. If the colleges were to be restricted to their existing single purpose of producing teachers, they were clearly in for substantial contraction and they would have spare student capacity. The closure of some colleges or the under-utilization of all colleges at a time when higher education provision needed to be expanded would be a gross waste of expensive capital assets. Lord James and his colleagues began their work at a moment when the statistical consequences of the roaring sixties were coming home to roost and when the colleges were demanding a higher education function not necessarily inextricably involved with the training of teachers.

The third major problem embracing and subsuming the aspirational and the numerical problems of the colleges was the forecast demand for higher education, the bare calculations of which were set out in *Education Planning Paper No. 2*[10]—727,100 full-time students in higher education by 1981. Despite the crisp forecast tables of student numbers up to 1980/1 in various sectors of higher education, the foreword made it clear that the vital question of how the numbers should be distributed over the higher education population map was still open. An even more open question was how the needed expansion could be financed. The paper rightly did not attempt to say what proportion of the Gross National Product would be needed to finance such an expansion since it had no means of knowing what the GNP might be in the seventies. It did, however, state that in order to cope with the predictions on existing assumptions of distribution without increasing the share of national resources devoted to higher education an annual growth rate in the GNP of between 5 and 6 per cent would have to be maintained.[11] This rate of economic growth looks increasingly unlikely and government faces the decision of either cutting numbers or cutting costs.

Cutting costs is more attractive politically than cutting numbers and no doubt the James Committee, based within the DES on the seventh floor of Elizabeth House, was aware of the political dilemma facing the Secretary of State. The advantages of a two-year qualification available within the system of awards in higher education had long been apparent to the DES. It was one of the 'thirteen points' which Anthony Crosland had put to the Committee of Vice-Chancellors and Principals. It was about the only one they did not reject out of hand. Financially a two-year qualification (provided enough students take it as an alternative to a three-year qualification) is attractive to government, and with certain stringent safeguards a strong case could be made for it on educational grounds. With annual costs per student unit running at £925 in colleges compared with £1,625 in universities and £1,120 in full-time advanced further education,[12] relating the cheaper qualification to the cheapest institution must have looked too good a chance to miss.

III

Given the simultaneous existence of all these factors it was hardly surprising that the James Committee should have related them in their proposals for restructuring the professional education of teachers. The colleges had made a strong claim for a higher education role in addition to their existing professional training function and had indeed suggested a phased course structure (2 + 2), in which education preceded training, with the qualification at the end of the first phase having recognized validity and transferability.[13] The teaching profession, through their various associations, had asked for greater responsibility in the training of their future colleagues and a substantial expansion of in-service training. In common with the colleges, they were also pressing for a system of training which ensured professional unity by establishing an all-graduate entry. The Department of Education and Science was hankering after a two-year qualification of some kind which would be a terminal qualification for a substantial number of students and at the same time a base which could lead to a variety of professional training. They also wanted to avoid movement of publicly controlled institutions across the binary line to swell the autonomous sector. Their interests here coincided with those of the local authorities who wished to ensure that the institutions they had provided and maintained stayed under their ultimate financial control.

The three-cycle structure of professional education which the Committee recommended—higher education, followed by professional training (partly institution-based and partly school-based), followed by structured in-service training—no doubt seemed to the Committee not only logical but also capable of meeting the major part of most people's requirements and/or vested interests. The total package was, however, offered on terms which caused a good deal of grief in many professional breasts.

To many whose exclusive concern was the effectiveness of the teachers produced by this pattern, the two two-year cycles seemed, where college students were concerned, to reduce professional preparation from three to two years. The separation of the professional cycle 2 into institution and school-based years implied for them not 2 + 2, but 2 + 1 + 1 in which 1 + 1 added up to something rather less than 2. It was also alleged that the advantages of concurrent education and training to which the colleges had been committed ever since McNair would be lost, and the end-on university pattern, which had been severely criticized, would become general.

Many have argued on the other hand that the bulk of entrants to the profession by 1980 will be graduates and for them the two-year professional cycle after graduation would be twice the length of their former training. For them 3 + 2 is infinitely preferable to 3 + 1. The loss of advantages alleged to be inherent in concurrent training may be more illusory than real. It is by no means impossible to make available within the cycle 1 stage, whether degree or diploma, options, courses or units which could have direct relevance to the applied professional studies in cycle 2. A number of universities have already made Education available as a component of first degree courses and these Education courses are taken by intending teachers and others with no such career intention.

Whether there is a lack of unity and coherence between the two years of cycle 2 will depend to a very large extent on the effectiveness of the training element in the school-based year. If during their time in schools, trainees are merely employed as may be found convenient and there is no attempt to structure this field experience, then this year will be nothing more than a long teaching practice with one day off a week for recuperation. If, however, financial resources can be made available to appoint an adequate number of training officers who could design the school experience and relate the day-to-day work of the school tutors to the work of the professional centres to which the trainees are

C

attached, then purposeful and relevant professional training could be developed.

The two-cycle pattern of initial education and training could be effective provided that the opportunities it offers are fully seized. Colleges, polytechnics and universities must be enterprising in the range of studies they make available at cycle 1 and ingenious in devising an overall course structure which would permit a variety of combinations of units, courses, or components to suit the various interests and career intentions of their students. Colleges, polytechnics, universities and schools must be given the means to create a genuine professional relationship between themselves in the interests of the trainees. Given that these requirements can be met, the implementation of the two cycles could be a significant move towards a uniform professional qualification and do much to abolish the invidious and anachronistic distinctions of first- and second-class membership of the teaching profession.

The real key to the long overdue solution of the problem is at cycle 1 rather than cycle 2. If the colleges are restricted to teaching for a two-year qualification (diploma) at cycle 1 while universities and polytechnics can offer a three-year qualification (degree), the first- and second-class syndrome will be perpetuated and sharply intensified. The college sector, though not necessarily all colleges within it, must be able to offer students who are capable of doing so the opportunity of taking a degree as their cycle 1 qualification. This necessarily raises acutely the question of the relationship between the colleges and other higher education institutions, particularly universities. The way or ways in which it is answered will determine the pattern of development in higher education in various areas and hence the national mosaic.

IV

College–university relationships have hitherto been mediated through area training organizations which with the exception of Cambridge have been the responsibility of university Institutes or Schools of Education. Area training organizations must meet the following requirements and discharge the following functions:[14]

   1 The members include training establishments and where

appropriate a university department of education.

2 The constitution of the governing body is acceptable to the Secretary of State and its membership is representative of member institutions and of universities, authorities and teachers in the area for which it is formed, and

3 It is formed for the purposes of supervising the academic work of member institutions, securing co-operation among training establishments in its area, advising the Secretary of State on the approval of persons as teachers in schools and promoting the study of education.

The Committee's proposal to remove these functions to a non-university body has aroused widespread concern and opposition. The university–college link has undoubtedly grown considerably stronger since the introduction of the B.Ed. and the development of an even closer relationship has always been sought by the colleges and the teaching profession. Universities have regarded the prospect with various degrees of apprehension: while willing for the most part to retain their pre-James responsibilities for teacher education they did not always see their way clear to being academically responsible for helping 157 very varied colleges to develop a wider range of activities. The package nature of a deal which would involve all existing colleges was somewhat daunting. At the same time there was an uneasy feeling in certain university quarters that some reconsideration of the role and function of universities was desirable and that some move should be made towards developing comprehensive regional networks of higher education institutions which would end the divisive and inequitable consequences of the binary system.

In spite of this, the James Committee (in the interests, presumably, of developing the professional relationship between training institutions and schools, and in order to develop the relationship between initial and in-service training) felt the functions of an area training organization would be best discharged by regional non-university bodies. It is difficult to see why a non-university body should be more effective than a university body with similar membership, responsibilities and powers. Be that as it may, the slender professional bridges between colleges and universities hinted at by the Joint Boards[15] and finally built by McNair have been recommended for dismantling. This being so, it is of paramount importance that the other bridges which the Committee indicated as possibilities should be looked at very carefully indeed. If the link cannot be retained at cycle 2, there is no reason why it should not be created at cycle 1.

The status of the Diploma in Higher Education is the fundamental issue. If it is an end-stopped qualification which leads only to cycle 2 and the teaching profession then the advantages of a two-year qualification in higher education will be irrecoverably lost and the colleges will become totally isolated in their 'third' and, by virtue of its limited function, third-rate, sector. The teachers educated in them will be more obviously second-class members of the profession than they now are and the primary schools they will largely staff will take on similar status. If on the other hand, the DHE could be developed as a transferable qualification which could lead subsequently to degree awards or professional qualifications in fields other than teaching then a range of possibilities would be opened up. The students would benefit by a wider range of choices and the structure of the higher education system would be able to develop a flexibility which could lead eventually to softening the rigid distinctions between sectors.

The attitude of the universities to the possibilities for their involvement which are inherent in the Report will be the determining factor. If they, in conjunction with the Council for National Academic Awards, will take the DHE seriously enough to share responsibility with the colleges for establishing its standards and will accept it as a defined stage to the award of one of their degrees then the system becomes open. By the same token the CNAA would have to regard the DHE in a similar light. It would also mean that the DHE could be awarded to students in universities and advanced Further Education institutions after two years, if they wished to avail themselves of it, and thus not limited to the college sector.

This recognition of the DHE within the system of awards in higher education would enable the diplomate who wished to do so to transfer to another institution for the completion of a degree course or for professional training of various kinds if the work he wished to take were not available in the institution in which he gained his diploma. The sectors in higher education and the endless problems of selection which these entail would loom less large in people's minds if movement between them were freely available on merit. The 18+ would be less decisive and divisive if adjustments were possible two years later.

As far as the 157 colleges are concerned this interpretation of the function and status of the DHE would help to solve some of the developmental problems which arise from their very varied natures, situations and circumstances. A major difficulty in planning a future for them has been the inescapable fact that they have never been more different from each other in their potential than they are at present. The unevenly distributed expansion of the last fifteen years has produced colleges which range in size from almost 2,000 students to barely 200. In some none go forward to B.Ed., in others it is over 25 per cent and rising fast. Facilities, functions and situations exhibit similar wide variety. A common future for them all is hardly practicable but participation in an awards system which permitted different colleges to develop in different ways seems eminently feasible.

The range of courses which any given college offered and the level of awards for which it taught would depend on the facilities and resources it could develop with the support of any regional planning authority to which it was subject. The variety of college developments within a given region could be considerable, each

Table 1

Cycle 1 (Higher Education)	Cycle 2 (Professional Training)	Cycle 3 (In-Service Training)
1 None	Teaching only	Short courses
2 DHE	None	None
3 DHE	Teaching only	Short courses
4 DHE → B.Ed.	Teaching only	Intermediate courses
5 DHE → B.Ed., B.A.	Teaching and allied social work	Higher professional degrees
6 DHE → B.Ed., B.A., B.Sc.	Teaching and allied social work	Higher professional degrees

The size of colleges could range from 400 students to 2,000+

one depending on assessments of the potentialities of each college and local and regional needs. In view of the various criteria which could be applied, defining all the theoretical categories of possible functions is not only difficult but unwise. It is, however, possible to indicate some examples of variety which could be developed. These varieties of development would do no more than hasten existing trends and recognize the hard fact that while all colleges are at present equal some are very much more equal than others. No college need be limited to a particular range of courses or awards for all time. There could be support and assistance for enterprise and initiative. The fundamental safeguard must always be that any student or serving teacher should have access to any course or award within the system provided that he can demonstrate his capacity to undertake it, irrespective of the institution he originally entered.

In this development of possibilities among the colleges, the universities have opportunities for major functions if they care to exercise them. It has already been stressed that degree opportunity at cycle I for college students must exist together with the DHE though only those colleges with appropriate staffing and facilities should teach degree courses and many of these would offer only a restricted range. Whatever the range, the colleges involved will need a degree-granting body to make awards to their students: there is little doubt that the vast majority of colleges would prefer that this should be the university with which they are already associated. How the universities respond to this desire of the colleges for their *imprimatur* will be crucial to the pattern of development of higher education. If they accede to reasonable requests from colleges well able to reach the appropriate standards they will develop much closer relationships with these institutions than anything which has existed hitherto. If the universities are uninterested in extending their function by making their expertise and experience freely available to developing colleges these ambitious institutions will have no alternative but to look to the CNAA or some other degree-awarding body.

A wholesale move by colleges anxious and able to undertake degree work away from the universities might spare the universities some short-term inconvenience but would hardly be in their long-term interest. The lack of relationship with other institutions and the non-participation of universities in the varied developments which will take place in higher education would undoubtedly reinforce the isolation and sense of remoteness which many people within the universities already feel is far too pronounced. If the universities decline the involvement which sharing in the development of the colleges would entail they would in effect be opting out. The result would be that the major expansion of higher education provision in this and subsequent decades would be diverted away from the university sphere of influence. The binary line would become more marked than ever and the universities would have played a major part in the firm demarcation.

Innovation and development tend to thrive in a context of expansion but are inclined to be limited in a restricted or static role. It could hardly be in the interests of universities to see their students form a shrinking percentage of the higher education population. The development of some university first degree courses in some colleges could help to preserve the balance and provide a fruitful ground for experimentation. The colleges have always said with some truth that they needed the universities: it might be said with equal truth that the universities in the future will need the colleges.

The fact that only a limited number of colleges would be seeking B.A. and B.Sc. degrees for their students might allay the anxieties universities have felt in the past when the colleges as a whole have argued for a multi-purpose function under university sponsorship. The James Report while treating the colleges collectively for the purposes of finance and administration clearly indicated differentiated functions for individual colleges within the common framework. 'The Future of the Colleges has always been a difficult generalized abstraction: the futures of the colleges is a reality capable of being worked out in particular and concrete terms.

V

The James Report is a prescriptive document where cycle 2 is concerned but descriptive at cycle 1. Here it describes possibilities and opportunities since the Committee had no warrant to prescribe roles for universities and the CNAA. It is to be hoped, however, that both will respond to the necessity of the colleges to develop a clearer higher education role as well as the education/training function they have had since McNair. In essence the requirements are few and simple. All existing degree-awarding bodies should recognize the DHE as a part I stage to the award of their own degrees. Degree courses should be available in colleges which have the appropriate resources to students who have the necessary ability. Students with qualifications entitling them to further study should have the right to transfer to other institutions if the course they wish to take is not available in their own.

The requirements may be simple but the effects would be complex and far-reaching. Students would have greater equality of opportunity and a wide range of choices: the system would lose its rigidity and the differences between the sectors of higher education would tend to lose their invidious distinctions. If the means can be created by which individuals can move across the binary line, there is likely to be less need and hence less pressure for institutions to do so. Blurring the binary may be the quickest way to make it invisible.[16]

> Changes in ideas often involve changes in organization. There are basically two attitudes to organization. One is to build up a structure which you believe is right—it might perhaps be called the architectural approach—and oblige people to work within it. The other is to go for a network of living institutions—call it the organic approach—where there is room for adaptation and experiment. I am myself convinced that the organic approach is better. It suits our way of life in this country. For the architectural approach you must be sure you have all the right answers, whereas good ideas can come from any part of the service at any time.

This statement by the Secretary of State for Education and Science, speaking at the North of England Education Conference 1971, encourages one to believe that the Department of Education and Science would not be unsympathetic to the kind of freedom and flexibility which intelligent and adventurous realization of the possibilities outlined in the James Report would permit. In the response to the challenges and opportunities in the Report the DES must play the ultimate deciding role by its allocation of financial resources. The colleges will never grow 'organically' or otherwise, nor be functional parts of any 'living network' unless they are given the resources which will enable them to participate as equals. A network can only be as strong as the weakest strands of the mesh.

Notes

1 'In the light of the review currently being undertaken by the Area Training Organizations and of the evidence published by the former Select Committee on Education and Science, to inquire into the present arrangements for the education, training and probation of teachers in England and Wales, and in particular to examine:

   i what should be the content and organization of courses to be provided;
   ii whether a larger proportion of intending teachers should be educated with students who have not chosen their careers or chosen other careers;
   iii what, in the context of i and ii above, should be the role of the maintained and voluntary colleges of education, the polytechnics and other further education institutions maintained by local education authorities, and the universities ;

   and to make recommendations.'
2 This point is dealt with at length by H. C. Dent in 'An Historical Perspective' contained in *The Training of Teachers: A Factual Survey*, Hewett, S., ed., University of London Press, London, 1971; and again in 'Contextual Change in the Education of Teachers', pp. 240–50, *Higher Education in a Changing World*, Holmes, B. and Scanlon, D. G., eds, Evans Brothers, London, 1971.
3 *Teachers and Youth Leaders*, HMSO, 1944.
4 *Fifth Report of the National Advisory Council on the Training and Supply of Teachers*, HMSO, 1956.
5 *The Demand and Supply of Teachers 1960–1980 (Sixth Report of the National Advisory Council on the Training and Supply of Teachers)*, HMSO, 1962.
6 Committee on Higher Education, under the Chairmanship of Lord Robbins 1961–3. Its report was published under the title *Higher Education*, HMSO, October 1963.
7 'Welcome trend to good honours in B.Ed. degrees', S. Hewett, *Times Higher Education Supplement*, 15 October 1971.

8 Provisional figures from Graduate Teacher Training Registry, 3 Crawford Place, London, W1H 2BN.
9 *The Professional Education of Teachers*, ATCDE, 1971.
10 *Student Numbers in Higher Education in England and Wales: Education Planning Paper No. 2*, HMSO, October 1970.
11 *Ibid.*, paragraph 6.16, pp. 31 and 32.
12 *Ibid.*, Table 14, p. 28.
13 *The Professional Education of Teachers*, ATCDE, 1971.
14 *The Training of Teachers Regulations*, HMSO, 1967.
15 Joint Boards of colleges and universities were established as a result of the Report (1925) of a Departmental Committee set up in 1923, under the Chairmanship of Viscount Burnham, by the Board of Education 'to review the arrangements for the training of teachers for Public Elementary Schools . . .'
16 Mrs Margaret Thatcher, North of England Education Conference, Buxton, 6 January 1971. Press Release from the Department of Education and Science.

The new polytechnics: their principles and potential

Patrick Nuttgens

Director of the Leeds Polytechnic

The new polytechnics have established themselves in a remarkably short time. Within two years of the founding of most of them it has become normal for newspapers and commentators to refer to universities and polytechnics in the same phrase. It is in many ways a surprising achievement; it implies that the polytechnics have established an identity in the public mind. And yet no polytechnic has yet, as far as I know, defined precisely its objectives or discovered its ultimate character.

I

The origin of the new polytechnics can be studied in the White Paper of 1966. It referred, among other things, to the polytechnics as comprehensive academic communities, to their involvement in all levels of higher education and to their being complementary to universities and colleges of education. A list of colleges was appended to the White Paper and the intention was that these colleges would be amalgamated to form thirty new polytechnics. At the time of writing, twenty-eight polytechnics have been designated, so that within the space of two years the intentions of the White Paper have been generally realized.

The typical polytechnic is composed of colleges of art, technology and commerce. In seven cases a college of education has also been incorporated. The colleges usually form faculties of the new institution, although in some cases the opportunity has been taken to split one or two of them so as to create a diverse and meaningful faculty structure. A common example is the extraction of Architecture and Town Planning from a College of Art. In size, the polytechnics vary from less than 1,000 to over 4,000 full-time students, and from less than 500 to over 7,000 part-time students.

It is essential to them that the part-time courses should continue and should form a characteristic part of their work. Whether full-time or part-time, their courses lead to degrees, diplomas and certificates. Many of these are national qualifications of various kinds ranging from degrees validated by the Council for National Academic Awards to Higher National Diplomas and Certificates and Teacher Training Certificates.

From the start attempts were made to define a polytechnic in some way more specific than the reference to comprehensive academic communities in the White Paper. It was not an easy task. The definition given by the Principal of Sheffield Polytechnic—that a polytechnic is any institution designated as such by the Secretary of State for Education and Science—contained a serious truth. For the origins of the new polytechnics were essentially pragmatic. It was a straightforward and characteristically English approach to a problem to base the necessary expansion of higher education on existing colleges in which the students could already be found rather than on the invention of another group of new institutions. The demand for places was inescapable. The predictions in the Robbins Report had already been exceeded, and it could be expected that the number of students able and willing to enter higher education at the end of the decade would double. How sensible and painless to up-grade a number of colleges and create new, comprehensive, multi-level institutions with large numbers and incomparable resources!

That deceptively simple administrative procedure disguised for the time being a more basic change that was taking place. You cannot change the scale and organization of an institution without at the same time provoking fundamental changes in its ideas, its attitudes and its underlying philosophies. While the polytechnics are therefore still trying to find their own identities, it is already becoming clear that they have attitudes in common and it may not be premature to ask if they have an underlying philosophy. That is not to imply that there should be a precise definition of the boundaries within which the polytechnics operate. Areas of educational endeavour are defined not by their boundaries but by their orientation towards more or less certain objectives. Polytechnics are not divided clearly either from universities on the one hand or colleges of further education on the other. There are obvious areas of overlap, both in their attitudes and in the subjects they teach. But I believe that there are several respects in which a polytechnic can be distinguished from any other institution.

II

The very existence of the new polytechnics implies the end of the general assumption that a liberal education is the only peak to which a higher education can aspire. Liberal education has a prestige and cultural significance in this country and in Europe which it would be foolish to attack. But the nature of a liberal education has changed drastically in the last few centuries. It began in classical Greece as a training in the liberal arts—the arts of speech and persuasion, grammar, style and rhetoric. It was modified in the medieval universities, in the renaissance academies and in the Enlightenment of the eighteenth century. It was effectively only in the middle of the nineteenth century that higher education began to polarize into education on the one hand and training on the other, reflecting the divorce of aesthetics and technology. While the industrial revolution created a need for training in the practical arts, respectable society moved into an area in which education could be seen to be unvocational and learning became more academic.

In the midst of the controversy between the Oxford dons and the *Edinburgh Review*, which had emphasized the importance of utility in education, Newman in 1852 gave a clear definition of a liberal education:

> This process of training, by which the intellect, instead of being formed or sacrificed to some particular or accidental purpose, some specific trade or profession, or study or science, is disciplined for its own sake, for the perception of its own proper object, and for its own higher culture, is called liberal education; and though there is no one in whom it is carried as far as is conceivable, or whose intellect would be a pattern of what intellects should be made, yet there is scarcely anyone but may gain an idea of what real training is, and at least look towards it, and make its true scope and result, not something else, his standard of excellence; and numbers there are who may submit themselves to it, and secure it to themselves in good measure. And to set forth the right standard, and to train according to it, and to help forward all students towards it according to their various capacities, this I conceive to be the business of a university.

Newman's account of the essential nature of the university as he saw it in the middle of the nineteenth century and his description of its principal aims must command respect. But his words are revealingly loaded; the intellect is 'sacrificed' to a particular trade or profession. In practice, of course, the universities themselves have, often unconsciously, moved a long way from that concept of a liberal education. But the underlying attitude of mind persists. If the polytechnics are to be regarded, in the words of the White Paper, as complementary to the universities, it is surely implied that it is respectable for a student to pursue a vocationally orientated education without any sense of inferiority to a student who is pursuing a liberal one.

That is in no way to deny the significance of the universities or in any way to criticize them. But it does suggest that the universities are not coterminous with higher education and that it has been a mistake to over-emphasize one aspect of education because of its identification with the universities. Higher education and higher learning are not the same thing. The university, in Leavis's capacious phrase, is 'a centre of consciousness for the community'. That is not the same as higher education. Education, after all, including higher education, has several purposes; they include, in Dr Joad's definition, '. . . to enable a boy or girl to make his or her living; to equip him to play his part as a citizen of a democracy; to enable him to develop all the latent powers and faculties of his nature and so enjoy a good life.'

The arrival of the polytechnics on the higher education scene is to some extent a corrective to a bias which has been marked for the last 100 years and is to some extent also the injection into higher education of a new and powerful force. It is not new in the sense that this argument has not occurred before. Controversy about the difference between education and training has been in existence for a long time. To take a point of view at the other extreme from Newman's, here is a comment by W. R. Lethaby in his paper *Education for Appreciation or for Production* of 1919:

> The proposition of this little paper is that English education, as traditionally developed and guided from the old universities, is not directed to production and to action. It is an education in appreciation and in a knowledge of what has been written. It is by its very nature retrospective, and at its best it is introspective—the proper introduction to a life of contemplation. It may be developed to so fine a point of 'pure scholarship' and elegant criticism as to become sterilizing and destructive. This type of education has become an English 'ceremonial institution'. It was the great class badge and the foundation for the old Civil Service and a

Parliamentary Career. At its worst, (and that was very bad) it was an education in 'side', 'bluff', and voice production; its inward unrealized function was to provide a myth of superiority to those who could pay. Since mail went out of fashion it became the defensive armour of a class. At its most acute point it seems to have aimed at inducing an ignorance of everything but the writing of sham Latin verse and prose. At its referred broadest it seems to propose some knowledge of languages, history, mathematics, and 'pure' science, with some understanding of what has been said in literature and philosophy. The aim of even Matthew Arnold was 'culture', the being able 'to move freely in the realm of ideas'. This was doubtless good enough in its way—one way —but we cannot all take the veil and retire from the often rough productive work of the world. Such education is nice and proper, and it may be that this type, improved and amended, may be preserved as leading up to one kind of human training—the department of archaeological scholarship and historical culture.

What should be done about it? Lethaby's answer was un-equivocal:

The control by academical scholars of the vast field of modern education must be loosened; for they start with an avowed doubt of all vocational education except that for their own narrow vocation of letters conceived in an historical spirit. General education has to be re-thought out as the preparation for various vocations, each of which is as cultural in its own way (more or less, and in some cases much more) as the vocation of scholarship.

In short, 'our education has to be re-orientated towards the active life'.

III

The most obvious re-orientation in higher education introduced by the new polytechnics is caused by their vocational character. In any course devised by a polytechnic there is potentially a job at the end; and because of the facilities from which the poly-

D

technics have been composed and the traditions from which they have grown, such jobs are likely to be connected with the professions and to be of direct value to society. That is not in any way surprising; it happens because the courses have many links with outside bodies and because the polytechnics are specifically geared to running part-time courses in demand in the locality. The satisfaction of local needs and the development of part-time work link a polytechnic closely with its surrounding community and that community looks to the polytechnic for the direct satisfaction of its demands. The efficiency with which this is done is well known; the Higher National Certificate, for example, is the most productive of all qualifications in terms of the financial return to the student compared with the cost of his education.

But to say that a place is vocationally orientated is not to say that everyone in it is being trained only for one specific job. There is a kind of education and training which is vocationally orientated in general as well as in particular. It is possible to set up a range of courses, with many links and overlaps, such that the students are being educated with a view to a vocation even if it is not clear what that vocation is going to be. In higher education, after all, the process of learning is one in which a definable subject is studied to such a depth that it is possible to develop from it general principles that will then be applicable in a situation unforeseen. The test of a vocational education is that it can achieve this result. It must be able to take a practical task and teach it to such a depth and intensity that it becomes in itself the key to a general education.

Inevitably, such a course is centred upon practical work and the kind of knowledge that is gained not only through thought and memory but also through the hands. The student has to learn to define objectives closely, to choose between alternatives and eliminate trivialities, to acquire the mental discipline of decision-taking. In this it may be wholly different from the kind of course which the traditional university sees as its mainstream. For it involves an education, of both mind and body, which is geared not to thought but to action.

That action, in the definition developed by Brian Gent of Leeds Polytechnic, involves the creation of new artefacts or relationships rather than the discovery of existing ones. As such it encompasses the work of the arts and of the professions, all of which are central to the work of a polytechnic. But it also means effective action. For the solution of practical problems it is necessary for a polytechnic to equip students with powers of discrimination and the relevant skills. They are socially valuable skills. The existence of a vocational opportunity is not therefore the primary criterion for whether a course should be initiated; what is essential is that it should come within the general range of vocational work. It is an aim wholly respectable in the history of European civilization and one which may now provide a necessary corrective to a bias which the universities have allowed themselves to suffer from in the last 100 years.

That bias has affected not only the kind of subject taught but the style of teaching that goes with it. One of the major disadvantages of the contemporary university is the inflexible structure and relatively narrow traditions from which it has grown and which effectively discourage experiment in the form and style of higher education. There appears to be something in the very structure of a university which influences the minds of everyone so that it is difficult to escape from its traditional strait-jacket.

IV

The style of teaching must be relevant to the educational aims of the polytechnic. I imagine that in most of them the kind of teaching is being re-examined; it already rests on traditions in the colleges of art and technology which are quite different from those, for example, of universities. It is to be hoped that they will build on those traditions rather than ignore them. As Eric Ashby argued in *The Times Higher Education Supplement* (15 October 1971) there is a case anyway for a change in the style of teaching in the universities. He quotes Alvin Weinberg on the difference between mission-orientated needs and discipline-orientated practices of the kind with which the university is usually concerned. 'The problems it deals with are, by and large, the problems generated and solved within the disciplines themselves.'

Unlike the traditional university, the new polytechnic is unmistakably concerned with mission-orientated work and that is why it must insist upon courses and studies whose very basis lies in the mission rather than in the discipline of which the courses are composed. It is in any case clear that few polytechnic courses are single-discipline courses. Their very mission-orientation or commitment to action involves several disciplines. But something still more significant is involved, which affects the very structure of the polytechnics. If the departments that run the courses are restricted to recognized disciplines it is quite impossible for them to teach anything other than the disciplines which constitute them. It is therefore essential to a polytechnic that its departments (or course organizations if they are not the departments) must be multi-disciplinary and will lack the neat and tidy boundaries which make the university structure in appearance so admirable and in fact so inflexible. It also follows that the kind of courses, especially sandwich and similar courses, must maintain their varied nature and develop—at different lengths and with different interruptions —in ways unlike the traditional university courses.

But against this, there are at least three respects in which the grouping of the colleges into polytechnics has brought them closer to the traditional university situation. It must be the case in a university, and one taken for granted without its ever having been discussed, that all subjects are equal. If a subject is of sufficient stature and breadth to lead to a degree of that university it must surely be esteemed as highly as the other subjects which lead to that degree. There are of course many differences between the universities themselves and on the informal network there are many differences in esteem between the subjects as well. But at least in principle it is necessary to establish the academic respectability of a subject before it is taught for a degree. I remember this happening in the 1950s in the case of architecture, which was new to most of the universities. There were traditional academics who could not bring themselves to believe that architecture could ever be a discipline or an intellectual challenge of sufficient calibre.

It has certainly not been the case in the colleges of which the polytechnics are composed that all subjects are equal. For one thing there are many different kinds of subject and course, full-time, part-time, short, long, thin sandwich, thick sandwich, leading to all kinds of diploma and certificate or sometimes to nothing. The heads of department were graded differently depending on the number of students and the level of the subject taught. And this carried into the field of esteem. It led to strange questions. Is economics superior to accountancy? Is sociology superior to social work? One of the tasks upon which a polytechnic must be engaged is asserting the respectability of the subjects which are its own strengths. Accountancy is certainly the equal of economics; social work is the equal of sociology. On this basis it is possible to establish the essential egalitarianism of a polytechnic and to develop a community of equals who are engaged in its teaching.

The idea of a community of equals brings the polytechnic closer to the idea of a university. And there are other respects in which the two kinds of institution may profitably grow more alike. For example, in the polytechnic a constant cry is heard about the need for time to do research. It can obscure the reality, which is better understood in the universities. I take it as axiomatic that any teacher in the field of higher education must engage in constant study of his own subject and the acquisition of new knowledge in it if he is to be able to teach competently. This is what some people call research; I call it study; a famous academic has called it reading and writing. It is not the same as setting up research projects to discover that more research is needed into the subject. It will probably take some time for teachers in polytechnics to acquire the habit of study or research as an automatic part of their work. It is in my view important that special hours and special people should not be set aside to engage in this activity while some *infra dig.* people get on with the teaching.

V

One of the questions that the polytechnics have to resolve in the next few years is the question of control of their work. They already supply courses leading to many external qualifications and for them external control is inevitable. But the kind of external control which such bodies exercise has been changing. Most professional bodies try now to approve courses as a whole rather than write the syllabus. In many cases they prefer to recognize the examinations of the institution as exempting the student from the external examinations of the professional body. With this approach the polytechnics must agree. For it in no way robs them of a proper power of self-determination and a degree of autonomy in their academic work. But it may take some of them a little while to reach that maturity; the traditions of many of the colleges of which they are composed do not encourage independence of mind and self-determination. In some of them teachers have grown accustomed to the slavery of external requirements and feel happy in the safety of such external controls.

It is crucial to their future that the polytechnics should rapidly acquire the maturity of accepting responsibility for themselves and for their studies. The controls from outside are apparently complex though in fact simple. Control by the local authorities, to which the polytechnics belong, is a control of resources; and it is not essentially different from (and is sometimes more generous than) the same control which is exercised on the universities by the University Grants Committee.

If the polytechnics acquire the necessary maturity in academic affairs, it follows that they should be able to award their own degrees. But I doubt if that is an urgent matter. At present it is advantageous for them to go through the process of promoting a degree with the Council for National Academic Awards and being submitted to the examination and criticism which is carried out by that body. Once the degree has been approved, the Council gives great freedom to the institution to run its own affairs, choosing, as a university does, the external examiners who act as moderators and critics. It will probably be several years before most polytechnics are able to undertake the major task themselves. It would not be a bad thing if some of the universities went through the same process before establishing some of their less convincing degrees.

A final comment is necessary about the development of teacher training in the polytechnics. Seven of the new polytechnics have a constituent college of education, which forms the basis of a Faculty of Education. It is possible to interpret such a Faculty as being a college of education incorporated into a federation of colleges which forms a polytechnic. In most cases this has not been the intention behind the proposals. The Faculty is expected to work, not as a separate college within a polytechnic framework, but as a service that uses the whole polytechnic as a vehicle for the training of teachers. The possibility of access by teacher training students to other departments and courses cannot be anything but profitable. They have often been far too isolated. But the incorporation of teacher training facilities could also be a determinant of the future character of the whole place. If that experiment fails, it suggests that the institution will never be anything other than atomized. If it succeeds, there is a possibility of cutting across the most rigid disciplinary boundaries; and that is the very stuff of a Polytechnic.

The Open University and the problem of inter-disciplinary education

Arnold Kettle

Professor of Literature at the Open University

Many of the problems facing the Open University in its early days are obviously peculiar to its unique structure and emerge out of its unlikeness to other universities. 'Teaching at a distance' involves all manner of difficulties which the 'conventional' academic can, no doubt thankfully, wash his hands of. He may pay some sort of lip-service to the potentialities of radio and television as teaching media: but he is unlikely to respond very intimately to what, both in time-consuming practice and academic importance, is the prior concern of those of us who work at the Open University: the production of correspondence material that is intellectually exacting and educationally viable. This, the average university teacher must feel, is altogether too far from his beat.

And, of course, in an obvious sense, it is, even though it seems quite reasonable to predict that over the next twenty years or so there will be a considerable increase in the use of correspondence methods in higher education as a whole. The purpose of this contribution, however, is not to rehearse the more peculiar problems of the Open University, either in principle or detail, but—in the light of a couple of years' experience—to explore what relevance some of our problems and practice have had to more general, and perhaps even universal, dilemmas facing those interested in the development of higher education.

In attempting this I want to make clear that I'm not unaware of the differences which our set-up imposes. Such problems as developing (maintaining isn't enough) high academic standards in an institution whose headquarters can never have adequate library or laboratory facilities, as providing research time as well as opportunities for an over-pressed staff, as achieving the sort of contact between teachers and students which is mutually essential: if I ignore such questions it isn't to imply that we don't spend most of our time grappling with them. I think, however, there is a rather serious danger in overstressing the differences. It can easily, in a dialogue between 'Open' and 'conventional' academics, let both off the hook.

I

The Open University—to illustrate this last point—is concerned with adult students whose educational activities are very much part-time. In a sense this gives rise to special problems. Mature students are different from eighteen-year-olds, not just in their educational demands but in their whole psychology and motivation. They are, for instance, as everyone teaching in Open University summer schools (including the 'conventional' academics) discovered, much more keen, more obviously committed; what the Americans in question-begging jargon call more 'motivated'. They are also, though in some ways rather shockingly respectful and gullible, *bound*, in the fairly short run, to relate their university work to the rest of their lives and needs in more insistent and thoroughgoing ways than younger students do, or even can. Yet this problem of the relation of university courses to the actual demands of life as a whole is by no means confined to adult students. It is behind a great deal of all student unease and disaffection, and—to be fair—of hours and hours of Senate and Faculty Board discussions on the reform of syllabuses. No-one imagines it is a simple problem and no-one with any sense thinks that either the pragmatic (vocational) or the purist (knowledge for its own sake) solution is the last word. My point is simply that in the Open University we are forced—whatever our personal predilections or preferences for a quiet life—to face certain issues which those working in the conventional universities, with their captive students and labyrinthine possibilities of personal retreat, can very often manage to avoid. If we have the splendid starting advantage of thousands of seriously committed and enthusiastic students we have also the knowledge that a drop-out rate indicating more than a certain reasonable level of human weakness or miscalculation could very rapidly bring the whole enterprise to an inglorious close.

The disarmingly public nature of the Open University's activities seems to me both its finest and its most vulnerable feature. It can lead to fear, pusillanimity and every form of vulgar concession. Or it can enforce a level of realistic tackling of basic educational problems which could be of value far beyond its own non-existent walls. There is no limit to either the potentiality or the corruptibility of openness. Like realism itself it can imply either the most contemptible and limited forms of cynical know-how or the fullest and most imaginative recognition of the possibilities inherent in the situation we inherit.

II

We are not unique, at the Open University, in operating on a Faculty as opposed to a Departmental basis. Within the Faculties a division into separate 'disciplines' is kept, though without any formal structure. That is to say, we appoint lecturers in, say, history or philosophy (though not necessarily in one traditional discipline) and have chairs in those subjects, but meetings of the staff in history or philosophy take the form of practical 'working-groups' to discuss common problems rather than institutionalized Departments, and all policy decisions are taken at Faculty level. This seems to work quite well in practice but whether it would do so if larger numbers of staff were involved it is hard to say. Much also depends on the sort of staff promotion policy adopted by the University: the old type of Department could very easily re-emerge without anyone consciously willing it. All full-time academics, including staff-tutors based in the Regions, are on the Faculty Board, together with educational technologists and our full-time BBC colleagues. This makes a total of something like sixty. In practice there is from week to week a shifting attendance of between twenty and forty. I myself think the presence of a number of lively and academically well-qualified BBC producers contributes very helpfully to the *general* operation of the Faculty. They bring into the work a dimension which isn't merely a matter of expertise in their professional skill. Because they are not in the technical sense academics yet are involved in intellectual and educational matters, they help the academics to see their role (and perhaps even themselves) a little differently.

All first-year ('Foundation') courses are operated on a Faculty basis and, in Arts, so are the second-level ones which are multi-disciplinary 'period' courses. But there will be single-discipline courses as well, especially (in Arts) at third and fourth levels. The important innovation, from the professional point of view, in our method is not, I think, that some courses are inter-disciplinary and some single-discipline, but that they are *all* planned and produced by course-teams.

Again, it's not easy to separate off principle from necessity. Since the University operates on a 'course', as opposed to a subject-basis (all students have to complete six courses which can be chosen, with minimum reservations, from any faculty, each of which runs from January to the end of October), it's clear that courses *have* to be planned and that no one person, however remarkable his output, could produce a course—including weekly correspondence material, broadcasts, summer schools, assignments and examinations—by himself. He couldn't even produce most of a course alone. And younger members of staff, perhaps in their first or second academic job, can't be expected to turn out more than a few 'units' in a year.

What does working as a member of a course-team mean in practice? It means, among other things, accepting personal responsibility for the planning and writing of a number of 'units'. But even in this context 'personal' has a 'group' slant, for the individual responsible for a particular 'unit' gathers round him a working-group of colleagues who have—at least in theory—some sort of special interest and competence in the subject to be dealt with. You can't have more than one person actually writing a particular piece of correspondence material. But you can have a set-up in which the writer can at each stage refer his drafts and ideas to a small group of colleagues for advice and criticism that is considerably more than a formality. You can also experiment in correspondence units which are themselves constructed as a sort of dialogue. Preliminary drafts of correspondence material, in our system, go to the members of the working-group, then a provisional draft goes to the course-team itself whose members have the responsibility of making further suggestions and criticisms before voting whether to approve the final draft. Unless the course-team is prepared—as has happened with us—to send back unsatisfactory drafts, the whole process becomes of course a mere formality. As far as broadcasting material goes, this too is sent in draft form to the working-group for criticism; when it has been recorded it is viewed or listened to by the course-team, who then have to approve it or not. We have voted to 'remake' a number of programmes.

I have already implied, I think, the other aspects of being a member of a course-team. It means that one takes part in the overall planning of the course, its structure and detail; it involves reading and commenting on a good many drafts of one's colleagues' work and taking these into consideration when preparing one's own; and it includes having a say in the final acceptance or rejection of the various complete elements of the course. It means, on a rather more detailed basis, accepting certain agreed limitations of space and time, and subjecting one's demands of one's students— reading requirements, essay-subjects, etc—to group comment and decision. In the end, as with everything else, the way the system works must depend to a high degree on personal relationships and goodwill; but there certainly seems no inherent reason why a course-team should not operate (as I think ours have done so far) without the imposition of any undesirable restraints on individual members. I would say that one of the major problems we have so far come up against is the difficulty of evolving a system in which useful and constructive criticisms can be exchanged *at the right time*. It can be unfair as well as impracticable to offer one's suggestions about someone else's unit at a stage when the vital decisions have already been taken; yet it is often hard to make responsible comments until the work involved is pretty well under way.

Obviously one can exaggerate the 'team' quality aspect of such team-work. The well-informed individual, relatively expert about what he is working on, will almost always carry his working-group with him; which isn't to say he may not at the same time gain a good deal from the team he works with. But even though in practice the system doesn't involve serious constraints on the individual academic's freedom of action, I think the principle involved is important and more pervasive than empirical evidence would sometimes suggest. In most university departments—at any rate on the Arts side—the lecturing system is an extremely hit-or-miss affair. Young lecturers get very little help in coping with the situation into which they are pitched. To quote from a letter in *The Times Higher Educational Supplement* (29 October 1971): 'The initial period of employment is called probationary, but if my own experience is anything to go by, probation is almost meaningless since no-one does anything to find out whether one does one's job adequately or not.' But the main point is an academic rather than a 'professional' one. In twenty years in a conventional university English Department I cannot recall having any serious basic academic discussion on a Departmental basis—beyond the occasional routine consideration of syllabuses and set books—on what I was doing except when I happened at my very first appointment to 'share' a course of lectures with the Head of the Department, an experience from which I learned a great deal. I am convinced that in many university Departments no-one really knows what is being taught or how effectively.

The 'principle' I've just referred to is not of course that the individual university teacher should be subject to some sort of control or censorship over what he teaches (one assumes we are all agreed on the undesirability of that), but that by and large academic effort involving a group of colleagues discussing their subject and reading each other's work is likely to be better than purely individual attempts to produce, often at rather short notice, adequate teaching material, lecture courses, essay subjects, exam questions, etc.

The underlying reason why teachers at the Open University have been on the whole not just willing but keen to submit their work to the sort of team-discussion I've indicated is, of course, that they feel it to be not simply a stimulus but some sort of an insurance. If all conventional university lecture courses went into print or emerged as BBC broadcasts, lecturers would be more inclined to try out their notes and notions on their colleagues first. There is no question that the chief emotion experienced by Open University teachers when they look back on their 'conventional' teaching days is amazement at what they then got away with.

III

The course-team and working-group system doesn't necessarily involve any considerable degree of experimentation in the nature and content of courses, though in practice I feel sure it encourages it. In the Open University the system operates in just the same way in relatively traditional single-discipline courses as in more complex inter-disciplinary ones. But its operation has, besides the academic advantages I've been discussing, the merit of focusing attention on teaching problems too: not just the methodological problems but the more basic ones involving such questions as 'What precisely are we trying to do in this part of the Course?' The most useful part of the role of our educational technologists has been the simple but awe-inspiring one of continuously injecting into course-team discussions the question, 'Yes, but exactly what is your objective here?' and not being prepared to take the answer, 'Oh, you know, just giving them some idea of what such-and-such is all about.'

It's also worth saying at this point that those of us who thought when we came to the Open University that we had removed ourselves from the radius of student reaction were totally mistaken. True we don't get the day-by-day classroom contact of the ordinary university; but we do get a more organized and, potentially, a more objective 'feedback' from our students (via the regions and staff-tutors as well as through more informal personal contact with students) than I think most university teachers manage to achieve. Again, what's involved here is less an organizational than a 'total situation' matter. Because I can no longer rely (as I used to) on my personal, almost purely subjective, impression as to how my teaching is going down, I am now forced to avail myself of some of the more objective reactions available (what proportion of my students, in reply to enquiry, thought my last radio talk 'very interesting', what proportion 'much too difficult'). I have found such information, pinches of salt and various reservations taken into account, both useful and chastening. Truly objective 'feedback' is—as anyone would guess—extremely hard to come by and one is often faced with a situation in which contradictory comments seem to cancel one another out. But, all this allowed for, I have no doubt at all, at the end of one year of practical teaching at the Open University, that I have at least as accurate an idea of student reaction to my teaching as I ever had in previous academic jobs. What one doesn't get, on the other hand, is enough opportunity to learn from one's students; and that is a serious problem.

You cannot have inter-disciplinary courses that are in any real sense coherent unless you have teams to plan them. This applies in *all* universities. If I approach the key question of the *value* of inter-disciplinary or 'broader' studies through a consideration of the ways they have to be organized this is because I believe much of the more high-minded discussion of value becomes a bit pointless and even self-indulgent if it isn't linked with the practical problems and also because I suspect that—as in life in general—the nature of the more theoretical problems involved only reveals itself fully in the course of experiment and practice. Blueprints have their place in assisting the process of change but

E

they are unlikely to come to much unless they emerge out of a widely felt need and the rough-and-tumble of experience.

IV

The Foundation Course of the Arts Faculty (like all the Open University first-year Courses) is indisputably *multi-disciplinary*. It contains introductory material to the disciplines of history, literature, art history, music and philosophy—the sort of material, that is to say, which might, in an expanded form, constitute introductory courses of a Departmental type, outlining some of the chief aims and principles involved in the study of those particular subjects whether in isolation or in union with others. There is nothing *inter*-disciplinary about this except in so far as students are obliged to tackle the rudiments of several traditionally separate subjects and will therefore inevitably have certain common problems suggested to them; but each subject is, so to speak, left to itself, and these 'introductions' constitute about a third of the course.

I think it could be argued (though I am not particularly concerned to do so) that even *this* degree of multi-disciplinary planning has its advantages, for the individual disciplines are at least forced to define—even if only in their own terms—some of their peculiar preoccupations. I am not at all sure that in single-discipline courses in most universities *any* guiding theoretical principles are ever enunciated to the students. I wonder how many students of English, say, at the end of a three-year degree course could answer intelligently a quite straightforward question about the *methodology* of the subject in which they are supposed to be specialists ? And in most 'general' or 'combined' courses no serious attempt is made either to integrate the various subjects studied or even to design the various separate components in terms specially suitable for the 'general' student. All too often he is offered merely two or three chunks of multi-purpose courses so that the man or girl taking, say, philosophy as part of a general degree, simply gets a third of a philosophy course alongside a third of two other disparate courses. You don't need a course-team to organize *that*. This kind of non-planning may sometimes be due to shortage of staff; but everyone knows that the unwillingness of a good many professors to sacrifice any part of their control to a supra-Departmental authority is a more potent factor in the situation.

The vocabulary of the problems I am discussing is itself symptomatic of the variety and confusion of thinking about them. 'Integrated' not infrequently means 'broad' (in the sense of a spread of *un*integrated subjects) or 'introductory' or simply 'experimental'. 'Broad' and 'general' have become—without further elucidation—almost meaningless epithets. The concerns that lead to the significantly widespread interest in 'integrated studies' or 'broader foundation courses' vary from a vague feeling that it would do students no harm to know a bit more about other people's subjects to a conviction that the present 'disciplines' are themselves intellectually disastrous. 'Integrationists' include people who want to bring several of the present 'disciplines' together; those who want to replace present 'disciplines' by something else; and those who want to ensure the integrity of existing disciplines by defining their role more acceptably.

I assume that the minimum acceptable basis of even a multi- (as opposed to inter-disciplinary) first-year course is that the different disciplines concerned should at least clarify some of their underlying approaches and differences rather than simply offer chunks of unglossed 'history' or 'English' or 'fine art' courses in which basic assumptions are never brought into the open. If one can't integrate one should at least be able to differentiate. In our Arts Foundation Course we are forced to do that, and then, on that basis, go some distance at least in the way of integration especially in the final section of the course which considers some of the main effects of industrialization on different branches of culture and, to some extent, on modern British culture as such. And in the very first section of the course we raise a number of very general questions relating to the whole area which might be subsumed as 'culture and society'.

I think the posing of such general questions, even if it remains a mere posing, is salutary. In most English literature courses in this country, for example, students studying poetry are never at any point faced with such questions as 'How did poetry emerge as a human activity?' 'What has been the *function* of poetry in certain specific societies?' Yet it's hard to see how any fruitful discussion of poetry can avoid them.

I don't want, however, to make excessive claims for our present

Arts Foundation Course or to underestimate the difficulties of evolving an inter-disciplinary method of work—let alone the more ambitious achievement of an inter-disciplinary discipline. Some of the Foundation Courses of the Open University are more fully the product of team-work than ours. In Science, for instance, the entire course-team takes responsibility for every unit and individual 'authors' are not named. In Arts we have adopted the formula 'prepared by XYZ for the Foundation Course-Team'. I think this is the product of differences in the nature of the subjects concerned rather than of a lack of team spirit. In Arts subjects, because a larger area of interpretation and speculation is involved, it is important that the student should be in some sort of position to assess his teachers as a factor in assessing his subject. What we have in fact produced is a multi-disciplinary Foundation Course which forces students to turn their attention to a wider range of 'subjects' than their personal choice and former experience might dictate and opens up some of the more general questions involved in inter-disciplinary studies.

The principal charges levelled against any form of inter-disciplinary courses (and ours have not been exempt from them) are that they are scrappy or dogmatic or both. It would be silly to pretend that the fears these charges imply are without any sort of foundation. The less they are integrated the more scrappy multi-disciplinary courses inevitably become. This, as I've already suggested, is the problem with many (probably most) existing 'general' or 'combined' courses in ordinary universities: Oxford's PPE is a good example. On the other hand, the more they are integrated the more they lay themselves open to charges of dogmatism or sloppiness, which aren't always so far apart as might be thought. Because of this it is tempting to confine oneself to a multi-disciplinary plan, hoping that out of the juxtaposition of various approaches and a fruitful differentiation between them will come a stimulus to the student to do his own integrating. I think this is theoretically wrong (more of which later) and in practice works, if at all, only with the proportion of students who are not the problem anyway. So one is back confronting dogmatism and sloppiness.

I do not believe these two commodities are confined to inter-disciplinary studies, and those who hunt (and indeed find) them in Open University Courses have, in my estimation, even richer fields to explore elsewhere and perhaps nearer home. But that isn't to dispose of the problems, which are real. The one thing to be said for some of our existing academic disciplines is that they are indeed—even in the more pejorative sense of the word—disciplines. Like the learning of Latin in the nineteenth century they train the mind, and the fact that the training may not be the most rewarding possible is, looked at from some standpoints, neither here nor there. As a teacher of English literature I used to think compulsory Anglo-Saxon a waste of most students' time. I still do; but after a certain amount of experience of later ('more sophisticated') forms of language teaching I can't help reflecting that those who did Anglo-Saxon at least learned something.

I do not think there are any easy cures for either dogmatism or sloppiness, though I think a properly-implemented course-team system can make dents in the one and help stiffen up the other. But the reasons multi-disciplinary courses seem especially vulnerable to the charges of one or both are themselves worth glancing at. It is partly because they are new and experimental and therefore inevitably offer the student a less secure framework than the older ones (sometimes well-tested, sometimes sanctified merely by time) to hold on to. This fact, though it has its dangers, has also its attractions: but I don't underestimate the problems it can raise for the more timid student. Another reason is that 'broader' studies are likely to involve both teachers and students in generalized propositions which the former may turn into dogmas and which the latter have insufficient resources to test. This, again, is a real problem but not one that can be met, it seems to me, by imagining there is some way of avoiding it. All teaching can become dogmatic and the more specialist sort is not more immune than the more general: and the difficulty of students in testing the truth of what they are told is endemic to what the educationalists abstract into what they call 'the teaching situation'.

There is, I know, a real problem about generalization. One of the main tasks in marking most students' essays in the Arts subjects is to challenge sloppy, untrue, misleading generalizations which would be easier to undermine if they weren't the product of quite unconsidered (not to say unconscious) assumptions and a superb unawareness that there is any merit in having at one's disposal a coherent structure of thought. The lack of any sort of intellectual rigour in most areas of the British school system exacts a price (though not the same one) just as inexorably as does the over-systematized French way. The same can be said, though, of English empiricism itself. Its merit of generating a healthy scepticism about intellectual processes in general is often balanced by a coyness about the inevitability of having generalized theories to be sceptical about. It is easy (and fair enough) to be critical of the teacher who foists his pet theories on to his students: but I think the ultra-liberal critic often tends to under-estimate both the student's resilience (not to mention impermeability) and the fanatic's own difficulties. Any teacher with a strong philosophical commitment quickly discovers that he does his cause more harm than good if his students have the sense of being got at. The dangerous dogmatists are really those who are unaware of the degree to which their own intellectual attitudes are determined by conventional assumptions which have become built in to a whole structure which claims a greater objectivity than it can sustain. What I am suggesting—not to beat about the bush—is that the basis of many academics' fear of 'integrated' courses is the suspicion that they can become the happy hunting ground of irresponsible generalizers or committed proselytizers. Well, of course they can. Just as specialist courses can be haunted by pedantry and the most sterile sort of academicism. It is more realistic to insist that teachers and students should try to be aware of their prejudices than that they should not have any.

The trouble with 'integrated' courses is partly that they can come to grapple with questions that the more conservative academic is not yet prepared to cope with on any but his own well-chosen terms (the whole complex area of the relations between social development and ideas, for instance) and, worse still, they are liable to challenge the specialist on his own ground. This is, admittedly, a hell of a problem. Anyone who has worked in any sort of inter-disciplinary course-team or co-ordinating committee knows very well that, given a little basic good-will, things tend to go smoothly enough as long as in the last resort everyone kow-tows to the professor of history in 'matters historical' or to the professor of economics when his 'field' is under consideration. And you may well succeed (you may well *have* to) in establishing a viable inter-disciplinary course without antagonizing beyond the academic decencies your Subject-Heads.

Yet it would be disingenuous not to recognize that somewhere behind or below the civil negotiations and the exchange of minor intellectual concessions, lies simple, brute fear. For what is an expert who has lost his expertise or a professor stripped of his Departmental veto ?

I am not, of course, suggesting that the introduction of inter-disciplinary or common courses need have consequences quite so dramatic or upsetting. But experience suggests that anyone who is really prepared to work consistently in our universities for something in the way of an inter- or supra-departmental structure might as well recognize early on that he is up against some pretty well-entrenched and tactically experienced interests with a formidable selection of high moral and academic principles at easy command.

V

It would be very surprising if, in the Open University, we had managed to do more than scratch the surface of the problem of achieving a more satisfactorily integrated approach to higher education. It is much harder to be inter-disciplinary than multi-disciplinary and harder still to carry to their logical conclusion the aspirations which lead people to hanker after an inter-disciplinary approach. For what is behind these aspirations is, I am sure, a deep-rooted and just suspicion of the very disciplines that we are seeking to integrate. If those disciplines are themselves unsatisfactory—not just too narrow and fragmented but more fundamentally vulnerable—then it isn't going to help much to try and integrate them. You are as likely to integrate their limitations as their strengths. That is why I wrote, a few paragraphs back, that it is an illusion to imagine that students can be expected to do their own integrating unaided: the truth is that nothing in their education or training—itself based on the conception of *separated* disciplines—will have prepared them for this particular task. On the contrary, most of the prejudices they have picked up are likely to operate in the opposite direction. Yet, significantly, the aspiration for something different remains, cropping up decade after decade in one form or another ranging from the mild desire for 'broader courses' to the militant demand to change the very structure of university organization.

The case against the present Departmental structure of universities, with the intellectual disciplines it implies, is not basically that the students ought to be trained in more of the existing 'subjects' but that they should be trained in none of them. The most fundamental and convincing case for a different sort of structure isn't that the present Departments give the students too much of a good thing but too much of a bad one. In other words it's the disciplines themselves that are misconceived, that the present tendency to abstract, say, economics or philosophy or English as though it *could* ever be an autonomous 'discipline' is bad, above all, for economics, philosophy and English. That isn't to say that all areas of knowledge and study are alike or can be treated the same way, that there aren't real distinctions to be made between Arts and Sciences, that abstraction can be avoided, or that economists, say, don't have to develop special skills which are much less relevant to, say, literary critics. But once the special skills and relevances connected with certain subjects become thought of as the essence of the subjects themselves, once pseudo-scientific claims are made for areas of study to which the claims of science are not appropriate, once subjects are taught as though their real peculiarities are more important than their contribution to a common body of knowledge and experience, then the rot sets in, not just for the unfortunate student trying to make sense of an almost infinitely complex world, but for the subjects themselves. Abstraction, instead of being recognized as a necessary strategy to make more manageable the immensity of the total problem, is seen as an end and a virtue in itself. Philosophy becomes something for philosophers, economics for economists, English literature for those with degrees in it. We hand over the essential value judgments to people whose high-grade blinkers are specially designed to prevent their getting an overall view.

VI

I know very well that it is easier to state this problem than to solve it and I am certainly not claiming that the Open University has discovered the vital clue to an inter-disciplinary discipline, though I think course-teams help. On the content of inter-disciplinary courses it would seem to be less essential (as well as less likely) to agree on the more theoretical lines of approach than to establish a minimum common aim. If one can agree that all subjects or topics within any course should be taught in the light of their origins, functions and developments one has got some way towards the sort of approach likely to throw up links between the existing disciplines rather than increase divergences of method. My own conviction is that in the Arts and Social Studies the key to a more unified and unifying discipline is an historical approach, and one of the many stumbling blocks the low priority given in many history Departments to the evoking of a sense of what historical development means.

Inter-disciplinary courses can be valuable, despite the intrinsic difficulties of trying to integrate what was intended to differentiate, because they are, in most sorts of university practice, the only immediately feasible way of counteracting the alternative of excessive specialization and because at least they bring people together to talk things over. As such their very existence becomes an earnest of some sort of attempt to meet the felt need that is at the basis of the whole question I have been discussing—the felt need of intelligent and able people (whatever their age or formal qualifications) to acquire a higher education which, without being limited to vocational or technical training, is linked with the actual needs and problems of a world that transcends Departmental or even Faculty divisions.

The structure of a morally committed university

A. B. Pippard

Cavendish Professor of Physics at Cambridge University

At times it seems as if one can hardly pick up a newspaper without reading that yet another public speaker has predicted the end of civilization as we know it within a few years. It would indeed be dangerous to pretend that the perils are imaginary, but at the same time one should attempt some measure of perspective and recognize that with all its faults Western industrial civilization probably provides a better mode of life for the average man and woman, and certainly for the average child, than was ever possible before. It is true we may have passed the peak, but if so, only by a few years, and it is surely not unreasonable to hope that there is a chance, after so many centuries of upward striving, that the subsequent downfall can be delayed long enough to allow a serious attempt to prevent it ever occurring.

I

It is all too easy for a physicist to delude himself that his analytical methods may be applied to the examination of society, and if I appear to fall into this trap it is only because physics provides me with convenient models. No physical system imitates the infinite variety of a social group, and if it did it would be unanalysable, but we may nevertheless discern in mechanical toys certain characteristics that give clear warning of the likely occurrence of similar characteristics in the real world of people. As a scientist I naturally use, in my private attempts to come to terms with what goes on around me, those concepts that professionally I understand fairly well and derive great enjoyment from; and I would see all students of science encouraged to do the same, even while they are left in no doubt that at best science can provide hints and not answers. The seesaw of politics, the pendulum of change, these are catchphrases that by now are but empty clichés; yet to the scientific student of seesaws and pendulums they have a rather sinister undertone. If you disturb a pendulum it tries to return to its state of equilibrium but overshoots the mark and then, left to itself, oscillates with less and less vigour before finally coming to rest. If, however, observing the overshoot you make an attempt to control it and damp down the oscillations, for example by tapping the pendulum back towards the centre as soon as it shows signs of overshooting, you are more likely to build up stronger oscillations than to stabilize the system. Successful control requires considerable delicacy in choosing the right moment to give the right tap. And something similar can surely be recognized in social affairs.

The manifest progress towards better conditions that has been observed over centuries has led to a naïve view, commonly held though not perhaps acknowledged, of progress as an orderly movement towards an ideal state which, being seen to be good, will be stable. But in recent years more and more people, and not just the elderly, have felt the hollowness of this view; it is as if, to change the analogy, climbing uphill towards the distant and delectable mountains we have found ourselves reaching an insignificant lower peak and have then been unable to prevent ourselves running headlong down the other side. The natural response is either to pretend that we were not making for the mountains anyhow, or to try to get back on to our little peak. Leaving aside the former, the rejection of previously accepted standards, we may see the latter reaction as not dissimilar to the tapping of the pendulum, and the outcome may well be the same. Repression of tendencies away from a previous and better state of affairs is more likely to set the system into oscillation than to produce stability. This may not be altogether bad—if impetuous reaction to change, taking little account of the vastly complicated nature of the process involved, is unlikely to achieve its object, perhaps a more delicate control would do the trick and establish a state of equilibrium. But would the majority necessarily find this acceptable? The concept of intelligent rulers gently exerting such controls as will stabilize the system is all too reminiscent of Huxley's *Brave New World*, and for many the idea of stability is hardly to be distinguished from intellectual, moral and social death.

II

It is probably not profitable to pursue the mechanical analogy further as a model of general social dynamics, but to turn to limited and specific problems where the model is more directly appealing. The example that deserves notice in the present context concerns the part universities have played in the training of scientists, particularly the way in which, over the last twenty-five years, crude analyses, leading to even cruder attempts at control, have helped to induce the present crisis. At the end of the war the benefits seen to have been conferred by science, in the anomalous circumstances of rapid technological development without thought of cost, were responsible for a determined move to increase the number of trained scientists and engineers in the country. The Barlow report[1] recommending the expansion of university science departments filled an obvious need and its implementation was successful. Some fifteen years afterwards, Zuckermann[2] was warning of the danger of saturation, but the means by which he acquired his evidence carried no conviction with academic scientists[3] whose chief concern was how to maintain teaching quality at a time of rapid university expansion, when the number of new posts outnumbered the competent graduates available. What we failed to worry about at that time was what to do with the new wave of graduates from the enlarged universities, and it was only with the publication of the Swann report[4] that the real danger of over-production of qualified professional scientists became apparent. It is worth remarking that the Swann Committee received evidence, sometimes passionately expressed, of the failure of the best graduate scientists to enter industry, yet within two years of the publication of the report these very scientists found themselves unwanted either in universities or in industry. It is easy to criticize employers for recognizing only short-term imbalances and demanding instant adjustment from an educational system with an inbuilt time-lag of six years between a student's career decision and his graduation; but before doing so one should also recognize that the universities' insensitivity to these complaints was not in general based on anything more respectable than indolence. In this case, however, indolence, if not meritorious, was a sounder response than hasty remedial action. For our mechanical analogue shows that a system with inherent time-lags, if too firmly committed to the immediate rectification of imbalances, is almost inevitably set on a course of ever-increasing oscillation.

I hope I have not implied that the physicist or the control engineer has any special secret for really understanding affairs of this sort which is denied to experts in other disciplines. But he can give warning from his experience in the simple domain of mechanics about how the control of a system that is prone to oscillate is normally too delicate a matter to be left to the whim of the moment. It demands a study of trends to allow the control to be injected at the appropriate moment and with the appropriate strength. If this is so in simple systems, it is probably even more so in complex systems of which the whole social organism is about as elaborate an example as one could conceive. Moreover, the very nature of the way in which controls are normally imposed, without detailed analysis of trends, even if this could be provided in the time available, by democratic pressure forcing governments to act in the only way left open to them, suggests that oscillations in the social body are to be expected as the norm, and indeed, as I have suggested, that we should not try to produce too great a measure of stability.

The question is whether somewhere between catastrophic oscillation and total stability there lies something like the analogue of controlled oscillation in which the structure of society is constantly changing, with different ideologies and aspirations exchanging power, yet never running wholly out of control towards the break-up that present day pessimists are so confident is about to happen. One cannot, of course, answer this question with any assurance, but it is my view that with the means of destruction available and the toleration of their existence by the majority, the forces at present moulding public opinion, through the news media in particular, are too powerful and too capricious to prevent catastrophe; indeed, by promoting concerted response to events they will encourage it. One should not, however, give up hope that a succeeding generation will be impelled by a little more knowledge and a little more fear to mitigate its ambitions and institute a more rational and gentler control such as will maintain something of the quality that makes the present age a landmark in human progress. This is a tall order, but in a sense circumstances are playing into our hands, if only we are farsighted enough to recognize the fact and act accordingly.

The demand for ever-increasing higher education makes it possible in principle for the universities and other higher institutions to attempt to educate a new generation into some measure of awareness of how critical the situation is (this is not difficult, for students are more ready than their elders to play intellectually with the idea of catastrophe) and at the same time try to engage their minds on the analytical and constructive techniques which might be brought to bear in changing the instability into one of controlled change. For this educational programme to succeed, an unprecedented change of heart is needed on the part of the educators themselves. There is a genuine intellectual difficulty in accepting that although we do not know how to proceed to solve a great and urgent problem, we may still have some ideas about how to educate intelligent students in such a way that their minds are not precluded from finding a solution. For this and other less creditable reasons the academic, especially if he is a scientist or engineer, finds it more satisfactory to follow along the lines that he has been brought up to believe are right, that is to train professionals to do the same sort of work and to embrace the same sort of ideals as he does himself. And if in response to the Swann report or the pleas of industrial employers he envisages wider horizons than these, he is usually satisfied with his adventurousness if he can advocate a smattering of general education in the courses he provides for scientists, so as to fit them for incorporation in the existing scheme. Yet this is surely too shortsighted an objective; it is all too easy for the academic whose primary interest is not in everyday affairs to assent to the views of the industrial employer whose view of society is basically economic, and who sees the cure for all ills to lie in the expansion of our economy. He may be right, but to believe it without question is possibly to prejudge the issue in a literally fatal way. For though it may well be that expansion of the economy will prevent an immediate breakdown of the country's way of life, the effect may be to head it in a direction which will only postpone the ultimate breakdown and make it many times worse when it comes. If we are to educate scientists and others to take an interest and play a practical part in maintaining the fabric of society, we must surely encourage them to look, if they can, at society as a whole, to criticize it as rational and deeply involved citizens and not simply as individual technicians, each concerned to optimize his personal sector. To espouse the latter course is to leave the essential decisions either to chance, as at present, or to the scientifically illiterate. In a civilization which is totally dependent on sophisticated science and technology, this is surely not an acceptable way of control.

It is not too difficult to produce an adequate number of professional experts. This is what the universities know how to do and, like the magic in the hands of the sorcerer's apprentice, they will continue to do it long after saturation of the need has been reached. It is a terrifyingly more difficult task to initiate the

F

growth of a scientifically literate population, capable of exercising rational and imaginative judgment in schools, in the civil service, in local government, everywhere in fact where persuasion and power in future are likely to reside in the hands of those with a higher education. This is the programme which, if only it could be carried out successfully, could turn us away from the paths of self-destruction into new and more beneficent ways. To hope that we have the time, the ideas and the will to educate coming generations to a more responsible attitude than our own may seem wildly visionary and certainly is not a hope to be entertained unless all else has failed; but faced with the real possibility that all else will fail, we must clutch at any straw and would be failing in our duty if we did not do so.

It would be the most stupid folly to pretend that any specific action we take has a high chance of success; if success should come, it will almost certainly come in a different guise from what we have expected and worked for. Our task therefore, if we are not to give up and let things take their course, is to plan without hope, since this is the best safeguard from relapse into despair when we see our hopes are not realized or delayed into what seems a quite intolerably distant future. Planning on this scale does not involve a fixed objective but, within a very general pattern, the seizing of every opportunity for improvement and the refusal to see each successive reverse as an indictment of what has already been achieved.

To ask the intellectual leaders in the universities and elsewhere to see their task in so frankly moral a light is a reversal of what has come to be assumed as the function of universities. The concept of academic freedom has too often been taken as the right to think any thoughts without worrying about putting them into action, or possibly preventing them being put into action, and this perhaps has been the natural response to the pressures of earlier days when the universities were under obligation from Church and State to maintain certain formal standards and subscribe unflinchingly to certain authoritarian dogmas. What I am suggesting here however is a far more difficult morality than is involved in keeping to the rule book. It is rather a creative morality that is prepared to look facts and ideas in the face and recognize that in the end it may not be enough to admit that opinions differ and that the matter must wait for more information or further discussion by experts. The Free University, relieved of the pressures of Church and State, was a fine and necessary institution; perhaps it must now make way for the Committed University. It is not enough to recognize that there are two sides to every question, when expedience and the general good demand that one shall be chosen and the other rejected. This is something which we find very hard to do, possibly because we who have chosen the academic way of life are often enough frightened of the responsibility involved in making fundamental decisions, and have found ourselves sufficiently talented to achieve respected positions where our fears can be decently hidden under a cloak of learning. But there may be, indeed there must be, among the student body many to whom action comes more readily than the nice weighing of pros and cons; in subjecting students to the atmosphere of a university we are unconsciously instilling in them those academic ideals of detached inquiry which are admirable in the few, but in the many amount to collective irresponsibility.

Seen from this angle, my proposal strikes at the very roots of the academic establishment; without being dramatic or flamboyant, it aims at promoting a peaceful revolution, and if this is so we need not be surprised if the technique by which the change is to be effected must be in itself somewhat revolutionary, or perhaps one should say surgical. There is no point in being alarmed at the thought of revolutionary techniques being applied to our intellectual life, when socially and economically we are in the throes of a major revolution. Whatever happens, there can be no return to the golden days not so long ago when the rich were cultivated and the limitations of the media of communication spared them the sight of the all-too-uncultivated poor. Whether we look back longingly to the age of Pericles or the Renaissance or even Edwardian England, these are false ideals which we must hope to replace by something to which future generations will look back with the same nostalgic longing. And at the crisis of change we in the universities surely have our part to play.

III

I have already made proposals about major structural changes in the nature of university courses, and if the transition from high-flown generalities to humdrum mechanisms may seem abrupt, let us remember that we do not know the end towards which we work and can only at best set up a structure from which we may hope the end may be discovered by self-revelation. For the rest of this article, therefore, I shall concentrate on structural matters and discuss in some detail a few of the points that have emerged since I first suggested a 2 + 2 pattern for university degrees.[5]

Let me begin disposing briefly of one or two points which do not need enlarging on at present. First I must emphasize that the idea of extending the two-year scheme into what has been called 2 + 2 + 2 is very far from my intention. That the course work of some students will be extended to four years should not be made an excuse to cut down the length of a Ph.D. course to two. Research students play an essential role in the intellectual structure of a university. The truncation of their research to two years would ensure in most subjects that no significant results were achieved and almost nothing learned by the students, and it would not make any substantial change in the size of the labour force of trained scientists available, though apparently not wanted, for industrial work. Let us recognize that the three (or more) years of Ph.D. work in a university are the first professional appointment of a graduate of the highest ability and that as such the work, which is of a character unique to universities, is lamentably underpaid. There is, of course, every reason for doing our utmost to maintain the high quality of this work and to prevent unsuitable students from taking it up, but there is no case for deforming its character in the interests of saving a small amount of money. If money must be saved on research (and the case has not been made), it should be by reducing the number of research students, especially in those fields where they are ill-trained or merely used as cheap labour.

The second preliminary point is to answer those critics who ask whether the scheme should not first be piloted at Cambridge or at some other university. This is a most insidious criticism, for it can only be met by revealing that no single university would dream of exposing itself to potential disaster by going it alone. The proposed change in course structure is so fundamental that if it is not taken up by a number of universities collectively it will certainly fail to achieve a satisfactory form and will harm any university rash enough to attempt it. Moreover, it is a basic principle in the scheme that students should be encouraged to move, after the first two years of general education, to whatever institution is best suited for the second two years of specialist work. Even if the instinct for self-preservation were absent, it would still be necessary for a number of universities to co-operate so that the specialist courses were not unnecessarily proliferated, as they often are now, to the detriment of their quality. The problem exposed here is the conflict that is inevitable when a major change is proposed; the genuine apostles of gradualism are supported by the much larger forces of inertia in preventing anything from taking place until a crisis precipitates panic measures. It is only the firm belief that a crisis is imminent that persuades me to propose the sort of co-operative course of action that is anathema to the majority of right-thinking academics.

The final preliminary point is to rebut the suggestion that it is proposed to cut down the degree course from three years to two. On the contrary, it is proposed to increase it from three years to four. There are very few university teachers who in their hearts would not agree that of today's students one-third at least could have gained as much, and probably with more satisfaction, out of two years of a properly devised course. In the context of a proposed doubling of the university population (and when I use the word 'university' I always mean the higher education sector), for two-thirds of the students to have a two-year course and one-third of them to go on to a further two years implies that a population equal to two-thirds of the present university population will be benefiting from an extra fourth year. The proposals, in fact, far from spelling doom to higher learning, are expressly designed to save it while allowing the universities to fulfil the equally important role, which now they neglect, of developing the intellectual powers of a substantial non-academic fraction of the population.

IV

To proceed, then, to more detailed matters, it is obviously of great importance to have a fairly clear idea of what is meant by a two-year course of general education, and if I expose my personal interpretation it should not be taken as a blueprint. Proposals of this nature can only succeed by incorporating the imaginative ideas of everybody who is concerned to make the new system work. And in revealing my own views I hope to stimulate others to think of many more, and better, schemes so that our universities may become more diverse and allow for the development of all sorts of normal and eccentric talents which all too often at present are trimmed to the procrustean bed of academic orthodoxy.

My view of a general education is opposed to two popular conceptions, one of which is that it is like the old ordinary degree, that is to say, a conventional curriculum in science or whatever academic field is chosen, but not carried to the level at which it is professionally useful. Unfortunately, the way we teach elementary science is conditioned by the needs of the specialist and, though not devoid of educational value in its early stages, is by no means the best that could be achieved if we could only redirect our attention to the problem, with the needs of the two-year student taken as paramount.

A second conception of general education involves supplementing specialist courses in science with courses in economics, business management, or something else hopefully useful to the potential industrial employee. This has never really worked, nor is there any reason why it should. The disparity of attitudes is too great and the majority of students, whose prime interest is in science, will be exasperated by the need to waste time on what will seem irrelevant ideas, superficially expounded.

Both these concepts of a general education fail because they see the main-stream subject, which (only for convenience) I have assumed to be science, in the conventional academic light, whereas the basic need is to think out afresh the function of the main-stream course. The student who leaves after two years of a general course, without any expectation of employment in any field demanding a professional understanding of science, has no need to investigate the intricacies of Newton's laws of motion or to commit to memory the classification of invertebrates. It may be (for I cannot deny it categorically) that such studies are the only way of expanding the mind through science. If so, we have to put up with using elementary professionalism as the basis for a general education. But it is a prime recipe for losing many of our students out of sheer boredom, and personally I do not believe that it is the right way to incorporate scientific studies in a general course, especially if we hope to attract many of the uncommitted students away from the Arts and Social Sciences.

There are certain fields of science which can be understood to a considerable depth without a vast apparatus of factual learning or mathematical technique. Human biology and environmental science are two that come to mind, and both have the advantage of displaying the characteristic methods of scientific analysis in a framework which is relevant to the ordinary life of the student. Such sciences are admirably suited to illustrating methods of attacking problems, what sort of problems can be usefully attacked, and how the results of a successful investigation can be applied either to suggest new investigations or to practical ends. Simultaneously, the student may find himself applying more rational approaches to his own life and problems, so that what he has learned ceases to be academic in the worst sense and becomes a way of life. If this fusing of the academic with the personal can be achieved, the programme for the quiet revolution has already begun to take effect.

To put flesh on to this skeleton of scientific education demands greater space than is available, but a little more detail can be found in another article.[6] It is enough to indicate here that the conventional academic thread of biology or some other science is to be seen as the unifying influence running through a much wider range of studies; if the thread is strong enough it can hold a considerable weight of subsidiary studies such as will show the application of scientific methods in engineering and other ventures, and will illustrate the interplay of science with the economic and social factors which create the tensions inseparable from any worthwhile development, whether it be the introduction of a telephone system or the control of malaria by DDT.

This type of general education must (except for its central conventional core) depend less on lectures and practical work than on the reading of properly documented case histories and their discussion in seminars. No system of general education which proposes to operate mainly through lectures will achieve its end, if that end is the really worthwhile one of encouraging students to use their minds responsibly in situations far more difficult than the true academic ever contemplates voluntarily. No amount of predigested wisdom will help the student to break away from the built-in prejudices of his teachers; indeed the seminars which can achieve this end are those in which the teacher recognizes that experience is the most he has in his favour, but that when it comes to thrashing out difficult practical and moral problems he will contribute more by abandoning his normal position of superiority and descending from the dais to the discussion floor. His role is not to feed in the right answers, but to maintain respect for rationality—to inhibit emotional decisions while there is still the opportunity for intellectual analysis or further fact-finding, but to press for decisions when time is up and not let the class conclude by agreeing to differ (the traditional academic compromise).

V

Leaving aside the natural trepidation that will be felt by many, possibly most, university teachers at the almost indecent exposure implied by such a programme, it may reasonably be asked how the teachers are to find time for all these seminars. This is where organization comes in. If general education is to be a rather tightly knit structure of central core subjects, each with its related branches, and not just a lot of snippets brought together at the whim of the student from an almost infinite variety offered by the staff, it is possible by adopting a more systematic structure to ensure economy of teaching effort.

Let us put a few numbers to the programme. Imagine a university of the future with at any one time 10,000 students in a two-year course, that is, 5,000 freshmen entering each year.[7] If they were to be offered on entry the choice of one out of fifteen general courses (with the main core scientific, social, literary, geographical, historical, philosophical, etc.) there would be an average of over 300 starting each course and over 600 engaged in one or other of the two years of each. At what will seem to English university teachers a very unfavourable student: staff ratio of fifteen, we should have the equivalent of forty teachers employed on the task and, even if we proposed so unconscionably high a number as 200 lectures for each student in each of the two years, we should still be asking each teacher on the average to do only ten hours of lecturing a year. It would not be unreasonable to ask for an average of three seminars a week from each teacher on top of this lecturing stint, so that the staff alone, leaving aside the help that could be provided by research students, could organize 120 seminars a week, or one to every five students. If we were to take, then, a class of fifteen as suitable for seminar work, we have the means for providing a full lecturing programme and three seminars a week for every student[8] while maintaining only a light load on the teacher, and a student: staff ratio that would be highly acceptable to the UGC.

It is clear that by avoiding the proliferation of courses that will interest only a tiny minority of specialists, the problem of adequate teaching becomes much less formidable from the organizational point of view, though nothing in the way of organization, of course, will make the personal problem of good teaching any easier. It may be argued that fifteen streams is by no means enough to cater for the vast range of academic learning. This is undoubtedly true, and a large university that felt strongly about it could certainly increase the number without much extra burden on the staff. But it might prove unnecessary, if only the different universities were to put together their options in different ways so that the student was not limited simply to fifteen different courses but, at the time when he was wondering which university to attend, had a much wider range of choice.

VI

So far I have discussed only the general education in the first two years, but this need not occupy the whole of the student's time at this stage of his career. There are many students who know already that they wish to end as specialists, and there are many others who, even if they are not so inclined, have nevertheless a deep enough interest in some limited field of study to make them wish to pursue it intensively. The general course should therefore be supplemented by a specialized option occupying normally perhaps one-third of the student's time as against the two-thirds taken up by the general course. The student who had set his sights on becoming a professional physicist could then devote some of his time in the first two years to the study of physical science (though not, I hope, so narrowly as in many universities nowadays) with a view to being ready, when the time came, for an intensive two-year graduate course (the third and fourth years of his course work) at a university whose specialist course appealed to him. It is to be hoped that the choice of specialized options available to students in this early phase of their undergraduate career would not be so exclusive as to force every student to attempt some speciality, but would also allow those who had no intention of pursuing an academic or professional life to extend the range of their general education.

At this stage one must face up to a very real problem. Many students, especially among the most intelligent, have already formed a narrow enthusiasm and are apt to resent being compelled to spend part of their time on what they see as useless general studies. This attitude will be aggravated if those responsible for admitting students to specialist graduate courses insist, as they surely will, that the student's performance in the specialized options of his undergraduate career should carry far more weight than his general performance. Considerable care is therefore needed to avoid what has hitherto in this country been the stumbling block to general education, that it simply is not taken seriously, so that ultimately the general courses are seen as the refuge of the weak and the indolent. Yet this attitude is not intrinsically necessary. The organization of courses in the United States often enough holds back from his specialist studies the student who has a particular flair for a particular field; yet one does not hear many complaints from the victims of the system that they would have prospered better in a British university. Once a structure is established in which the necessity of general education is taken for granted, it will soon be found that the generations of students brought up in the shadow of that structure will take it for granted, and swallow their general education as though it were the most natural thing in the world, as indeed it ought to be.

Courses of general studies based on science, its methods and applications, its social, historical and political implications, need in no way be regarded as soft options. The problems they are concerned with are more difficult than the problems that a scientist normally meets and there should therefore be no feeling that time spent out of the laboratory is time wasted. It is up to the organizers of the general courses to see that this is so. Nevertheless, having said all this, there is still a sizeable residual problem. The talented musician or mathematician or scientist may be a highly eccentric person in the degree of polarization of his interests and abilities, and too rigid a structure may well cause anguish and harm to just those talents which are rarest and most deserving of sympathetic development. I believe, however, that a suitable structure for examinations and grants can be devised along the following lines, to allow flexibility just where it is needed.

VII

At present the student who is accepted by a university is virtually certain of qualifying for financial support if he needs it and this, one hopes, would remain true for the first two years of general studies leading to the bachelor's degree. But certain restrictions are needed for the following two years of graduate studies. For one thing, the number of graduates must surely be severely controlled with an eye to the country's needs for specialists. I should like to see public support available for all graduates who were accepted by the approved institutions, provided that they had reached a certain qualifying mark in their general studies. This qualifying mark should not be derisively low, but at the same time it should not be so high that every student has to strain to reach it. The good all-round student who is sufficiently talented to deserve a further two years of specialist education should be able to reach the qualifying mark without excessive effort, and the really talented student might well find that he can cope with the general courses in a good deal less than two-thirds of his time, leaving open more than one-third for the specialism in which he takes real delight. I believe that such a system would allow freedom of choice, particularly for the excellent who most need that freedom, while establishing a safeguard to prevent the admissions policy of institutions of specialist education from bringing general education into disrepute. Sordid though it may seem, at a time when the high-flown principles of education and the good of society are under discussion, to concentrate any attention on examinations and money, it must nevertheless be recognized that these two are the potent instruments for enforcing an educational policy and that, if this side of the organization is neglected or incorrectly applied, all the high ideals will go for nothing and the re-organization will be wasted.

The question of selection for the second two years leads to another general problem which is constantly raised in criticism of a scheme like that advocated here. It is said that all students will wish to take the full four years and that those who do not succeed in winning admission to a graduate course will see themselves branded as failures. It is obviously of the greatest importance not to allow such an attitude to develop. The first thing to do is to insist that success in the first two years shall qualify for a bachelor's degree, rather than a diploma or certificate carrying no esteem, so that those who leave the educational system after two years do so with credit and with no sense of having dropped out. We should altogether disregard sentimental protests that this will degrade the standard of the degree. We have only to look at its significance in countries so diverse as the United States and India to see that, internationally speaking, the bachelor's degree has no uniform standard. But in any case we are concerned with problems that far transcend trivialities of status. There is no evidence that those who graduated during the last war after two years at the university, or sometimes even less, have in any way had their careers blighted by the shorter period of residence. Provided the courses are well devised to stimulate the minds of the students, they will come out after two years at least as worthy of the bachelor's status as that substantial fraction who leave our institutions now after three years with their imaginations permanently impaired.

But to return to the bugbear of failure which is, I think, greatly exaggerated; we already possess a sufficiently close analogy to be able to see our way out of the difficulty. At present some 15–20 per cent of science graduates proceed to the Ph.D. Do those who leave the university without a Ph.D. regard themselves as failures ? Surely not. There are, for certain, a number who had nursed ambitions towards research, and who are deeply disappointed to find that their performance does not qualify them, but very few of these, I venture to suggest, go through life with a permanent sense of failure; it helps them to put aside disappointment that they have lived alongside research students and have seen for themselves that the nature of the work and the degree of devotion required for success are totally different once the undergraduate phase is over. It is indeed so obviously different that the majority of students know already that they are not suited to research. Something of the same sort of attitude could, and should, be encouraged at the frontier between undergraduate and graduate studies.

The general courses should be such as to allow the student plenty of leisure for discussion, sport and other extra-curricular activities, which are an essential part of the educational process. On the other hand, the specialist courses designed to produce professional scholars, research workers, doctors, technologists, etc., should be much more severe and demand more concentrated application than the first two years. Moreover, these studies, as well as research, should as far as possible proceed in parallel with, and in the same institutions as, the general courses so that the difference in attitude is made manifest. We should then find that a large number of students in their first two years would recognize in themselves an antipathy to concentrated academic study, and this goes not just for the weak ones but for many with quick and lively minds whose ambitions do not therefore automatically point to a specialist or professional calling. Ideally, the pitch of the specialist courses should be screwed to the point where examinations for entry are almost unnecessary, where indeed selection is by the students themselves. If very few who are unqualified wish to enter on these courses, and the numbers so wishing are not greatly in excess of the number of places available, the burden of selection by examination is lightened; moreover the pressure of uninformed public opinion still further to increase the opportunities for higher education is resistible.

VIII

This last point is so important that I shall restate it in different, but no less explicit, terms. The present demand for enlarging higher education is taking place simultaneously with, and in spite of, mounting criticism of the fundamental character of this education. It is the severance of communication between secondary and tertiary institutions that makes this paradox possible. If the schools knew, by intimate contact, what university life was like, a revolution in structure would already have occurred or, alternatively, the universities could have retained their exclusive elitism by being accepted in their chosen role. Surely we must guard against the further spread of educational demand if it arises out of misconceptions of the true state of affairs. Otherwise the enlargement of tertiary education will be followed by a progressive deterioration of the intellectual standard of what is taught (see, e.g., the syllabuses taught in many State Universities in the USA), and this will lead in its turn to stronger demand for graduate courses, not as specialist training, but as the means of making good earlier deficiencies. The way to halt this extremely expensive erosion is, as I have suggested above, to devise an institutional structure in which there is overlap at the critical boundaries; every stage of education should be embarked on voluntarily, in the knowledge of what it entails, and not in Gadarene ignorance. And therefore we who value academic standards should join those whose concern is the public purse to resist with all our might any attempt to solve the short-term problem by setting up two-year colleges, from which the fortunate clever may be permitted to proceed to a proper university degree. This course, so tempting when money and student accommodation are short, will in the end, if adopted, only make matters worse, and still more expensive to rectify.

But there is another reason for resisting any temptation to segregate mass tertiary education from the universities. It is on the masses that our future hangs, and if they are to be educated as they deserve, their education must be the concern of every citizen who takes these matters to heart. The time has gone by when the universities could be permitted to suck the intellectual community dry in the interests of specialized teaching and research; now is the time to insist that they shall play their part in devising and maintaining a responsible educational programme. If they are enabled by short-sighted policy decisions to opt out once more, we shall condemn the majority of the population to be taught citizenship without the help of that highly intelligent minority who in the past generated the ideas that largely controlled the development of our social structure, and who in the future must surely have a say in how we help our children to improve on what we were able to build.

Notes

1 *Committee on Scientific Manpower* (Chairman: Sir Alan Barlow) (London: HMSO Cmd 6824, 1946).
2 *The Long-Term Demand for Scientific Manpower* (London: HMSO, Cmnd 490, 1961).
3 *Problems Facing University Physics Departments* (London: The Institute of Physics and The Physical Society, 1963).
4 *The Flow into Employment of Scientists, Engineers and Technologists* (London: HMSO, Cmnd 3760, 1968).

5 *Ibid.*, Annex E. See also A. B. Pippard, E. W. Parkes, A. D. I. Nicol and W. A. Deer, 'University Development in the 1970s' (*Cambridge University Reporter*, *100*, 1269, 1970 and (abridged) *Nature*, *228*, 813, 1970).

6 A. B. Pippard, 'The Educated Scientist' (*Physics Bulletin*, *20*, 453, 1969).

7 This may seem large, but it is smaller than most of the renowned universities of Europe and the USA, and very little larger than Oxford or Cambridge. The small university is either expensive or mediocre.

8 Arithmeticians will observe that if the seminar size equals the student: staff ratio, the number of seminars given to each student equals the number given by each staff member.

Holes in the walls: university adult education

H. A. Jones

*Vaughan Professor of Education
at Leicester University*

The common man's idea of a university has never, so far as I know, been systematically charted but acquaintance with him in extra-mural classes soon begins to uncover the curious and shifting foundations on which his idea is based. Perhaps one is not wholly fanciful in seeing images of these in the successive modes of university building.

I

From the walled gardens of Christminster a generous-hearted don could sally forth to give Extension lectures to the common man and be rewarded with awe and gratitude (not to mention a princely fee: a fiver for a lecture in 1890 *was* money). But once back within his walls, lecturer and audience were on different planets and neither would think of questioning the fact. The civic foundations, deriving from a union of that Extension lecturing of the older universities and the active interest of the local community, opened a door for the uncommon son of the common man but their brick fastnesses swallowed him into a world as private as ever from the common view. Outside the walls extra-mural teaching grew and spread, with departments established to develop it, and through the Workers' Educational Association acquired a slightly guilty concern for the underprivileged. But the main stream of the university's life flowed on invisible from the outside world. Only on rag days were students seen.

Plate-glass seems different: it can be seen through. The new university towers stick out from the landscape, advertising wealth and inviting questions about it. Students are seen everywhere, hair flowing and thumbs waving, and their actions are news. Not only do their numbers include more sons of the common man but by their livery and behaviour they clamour to be identified as brothers of his other children. The modern university appears to be a visible part of the ordinary world, its doings tried daily in the courts of the media for judgment by the common man; who also now knows—and says—that he pays for it.

Yet the truth is still that the main streams of university life—undergraduate and post-graduate teaching and research—go on unperceived: when does the common man ever see a student *studying*? Moreover the pressure of demand for places means inevitably that universities are often felt by traipsing applicants and anxious parents to be aloof and heartless. The judgment of the common man on the nature and conduct of universities today will remain partial, founded on external appearances no less than his father's was founded on the exterior walls, unless he has the means of learning what university study is like. In an age when the demands of the education service on national resources are seen by many as insupportable while at the same time ever more candidates come forward with valid claims for extended benefit, it becomes imperative that the nature of a university should be understood as widely as possible among the electorate. Otherwise the cases for and against the universities in the arbitration of claims to resources are likely to be made on wholly wrong grounds. The argument for the universities' involvement in the education of the public has become political in a way that it never was before: it is the universities themselves that may now stand to benefit most.

It is in this light that the 'adult education' of universities may now have to be considered. The phrase is of course a term of art that has had different meanings at different times, none of them deriving quite literally from the words themselves. In one sense all university teaching consists of educating adults, as does much of further education and the rest of higher education. But the term 'adult education' has often been restricted to non-vocational classes and, in university terms, to formal extra-mural classes; or, even more narrowly, to classes in the 'liberal' subjects having an avowed social relevance. Definition has long been bedevilled by these false antitheses between vocational and liberal or vocational and non-vocational. University adult education must now be seen as embracing a wide range of learning situations outside formal degree work: post-experience courses, specialized and advanced courses, courses leading to certificates and other awards, conferences, symposia, seminars, as well as the traditional liberal studies.

But universities do much more than this for their localities. They maintain museums, for example, and planetaria, observatories, field stations and the like; they hold recitals and exhibitions; they provide special lectures; they run theatres; they staff social projects, surveys, and so on. Many such activities are a spin-off from things that the universities would want to do for themselves anyway. They simply allow outsiders to share in their enjoyment. In so far as these activities spread acceptance of the universities' values they may be part of the landscape of adult education and I should be the last to deny their intrinsic worth or their importance to the community. But in practice they may be not much more than spin-off, with an educational impact no more specific to the university than that of the municipal entertainments department. In this paper I shall be much more concerned with the universities as places of study and with the consequences of this for themselves and for the public.

II

The traditional piece of machinery for providing university teaching to the general public is the department of extra-mural studies. The term 'extra-mural' has long had its critics, mainly because any definition by negation implies a lack of identifiable features. Since an increasing proportion of so-called extra-mural work is now in fact carried on inside university premises, it becomes a less appropriate epithet than ever. But it enshrines a set of deeply-held attitudes in which the walls are palpable: inside—the disciplined legionaries, outside—the barbarians; or barons within and villeins without. Whatever the imagery the term is not of today. Small wonder therefore that a number of universities have chosen other titles: there are Departments of Adult Education at Hull, Keele, Leicester, Manchester, Newcastle and Nottingham; a Centre for Adult Education at Surrey; a Centre for Continuing Education at Sussex; a Centre for Adult Studies at Bath; a Centre for Extension Studies at Loughborough; an Institute of Extension Studies at Liverpool; and the Oxford proposal is for a Department of External Studies.

Ingenuities of nomenclature like this often spring from insecurity and there is no doubt that these departments have generally felt themselves to be inadequately recognized by their universities, treated as peripheral and starved of resources. A proportion of their working income derives from the DES under the Further Education Grant Regulations and this has sometimes been claimed as a factor condemning them to low esteem, especially as H.M. Inspectors are supposed to have a final say in what they may properly do. No other university department is subject to such inspection.

But there is equally no doubt that these departments have

grown in an astonishing way over the last twenty years, despite
the alleged indifference of many sectors of their universities and
of the central government. In the UGC Report of 1948 a sharp
attack on extra-mural work was set out.

> The advocates of the principle that extra-mural work should
> not in future be treated as a normal university function rest
> their case broadly upon the belief that, though undoubtedly
> great benefits flow from adult education, the extra-mural
> work done by universities is not of genuinely university
> quality, that it has never been properly integrated into the
> life of the university . . . It is urged that interest in the
> extra-mural work is confined to a small fraction of the
> internal teaching staff and the whole-time extra-mural tutors,
> many of whom necessarily live and work at places remote
> from the university, have little effective contact with their
> internal colleagues and are not, in fact, regarded as of
> equivalent status with them.

All that the Report had to say on the other side was that

> The extra-mural work of a university should be regarded not
> as a service rendered for the convenience of external bodies,
> but as a necessary and integral part of its normal activity.

But it was left to the individual university to decide just what its
normal activity was and how its extra-mural work could be made
necessary and integral.

That the work of the extra-mural departments did not then
wither away must be taken as evidence that there was something
necessary about it. Necessary to whom? To the university? Ever
since the 1907 conference on *Oxford and Working-Class Education*
which a shipyard worker galvanized with the assertion 'that
workpeople could do more for Oxford, than Oxford can do for
the workpeople', there has been a reiteration of this idea that the
university benefits from its association with real people and real
issues. At the level of the individual teacher this is profoundly
true: there is no keener stimulus to re-examine your teaching
methods and the assumptions of your subject than discussion
with a good adult class, and many senior academics, including more
than one vice-chancellor of recent times, have spoken with affec-
tion of the intellectual rewards they have drawn from their

extra-mural teaching. Indeed one may see here, rather than in the fees paid, the main incentive for university teachers to participate in it. But that the universities as institutions should have felt the necessity seems to me more difficult to sustain.

III

The needs must rather be sought in two other directions: in the adult students and in the departments themselves. Extra-mural work grew and developed, broadening out and taking new directions, because it was meeting a genuine set of demands which, when articulated, could be seen as compatible with the emerging self-concept of the universities. But the momentum to identify and articulate these demands came from the self-concept of the extra-mural departments.

These had grown up in the inter-war years when the most rapid development had been in 'classes for workpeople' organized through the machinery of the Workers' Educational Association. Though, as has recently been shown by B. W. Pashley, old-style University Extension classes of the type pioneered by James Stuart, Sadler, Mackinder and others from the 1870s onwards continued to flourish in many places, the tradition inherited by the extra-mural departments was of automatic university response to the organized demands of the WEA, chiefly for classes in the traditional liberal subjects and with some relevance to the need of the educationally deprived. The most respected form was the Tutorial Class, which lasted for three years, required regular reading and written work from its members and, although assuming no initial standard of entry, aimed at the achievement of a university standard by the end of the course. Here the universities' long attachment to the constructive criticism of society found an outlet in action. By 1939 there were 810 such Tutorial Classes in the country, with 12,491 students, and virtually all universities and university colleges were engaged in providing them.

This tradition is still confidently espoused in a few universities. After the second war, however, a number of new factors combined to call it in question, and the UGC Report of 1948, quoted above, summarized some of these. More important was the influx of new full-time staff, made possible by Ministry of Education grants towards their salaries. Where there had been 83 full-time teaching staff in 1945–6, there were 242 in 1949–50. These young professionals saw themselves as academics, committed members of the university community, rather than as missionaries to the underprivileged. If, as the UGC had said, some of them necessarily worked at a distance from their universities, enough of them have since achieved distinction, including chairs, in their own disciplines to rebut the charge of separation from their internal colleagues. They demanded decent career prospects and equality of status with internal teachers. So they were sensitive to accusations of low academic standards in their classes and often impatient of what came to be known as 'the mystique' of adult education for the manual worker.

For without much special effort on their part, the extra-mural departments now found that opportunities for academically congenial work were growing around them. There seems to be a permanent tendency, understandable and unexceptionable, for adult education to be sought out most eagerly by those who have already profited from the education service and this tendency, building on the enlargement of educational opportunity since 1944, has materially altered the constituency of university adult education. The emergence of new professions, especially those with an inter-personal bias but no acknowledged lines of qualification, like social work and various kinds of administration, was creating demands in many fields that had not figured largely in the old traditions. Here was a population, already familiar with the techniques of study, capable of discerning its own specific objectives, and often in a hurry, that knew the universities had something useful to say; and a number of universities energetically set about saying it.

In the process, the departments found themselves re-examining their relation to the universities. In the old traditions, the university was, if not an agent of social change, at least a resource with a moral obligation to be at the service of those who sought social change through the equalizing of educational opportunity. The health of a democratic society depended on this, and those who had climbed farther up the educational ladder had a duty to reach down to their less fortunate fellows. But not all departments of a university are relevant to such ends, and what the old tradition required, in effect, was that the extra-mural department should act as a critical selector, drawing out from the totality of the university the teaching resources that would contribute to this social purpose. The determinants of the selection lay not within the university but outside. This function was often defended as the creative, as distinct from the merely administrative, role of the extra-mural department. When therefore the UGC said that only a small fraction of university teachers were involved they were missing the point: the fraction of those in the subjects commonly taught extra-murally would be much more significant.

But a great deal of university expansion had taken place in subjects which for this purpose were irrelevant, and it was often in those areas that powerful new demands from a sophisticated public were emerging. What might be called the New Extension tradition grew up rapidly in some places in response. It derived from a quite different view of the extra-mural department's relationship to the university. The determinants now were the range of specialisms available in the total university, and the function of the department came to be the identification of groups in the adult population to whom any one of these specialisms might be of service. The objectives in this work are not social objectives but learning objectives and the length and format of courses have become much more flexible and varied, while the teaching is often much more like the teaching of undergraduates. Some universities have set up substantial and demanding courses leading to certificates and diplomas, while at the other extreme there has been a growth of short, intensive courses, sometimes for a single day, with highly specific objectives. To look through the annual report of a department that has cultivated this New Extension work may give the impression of rag-bag heterogeneity. That is what the Old Traditionalists would say: such an extra-mural department has ceased to have a creative and socially purposeful role and has become merely a set of switchgear. To which the reply of the New Extension would be that the variety is the variety of the university itself and that gives it unity.

IV

The universities that have followed the New Extension tradition most fully have found themselves in an ambiguous position. Because the tradition is that the teaching costs of extra-mural education are largely borne out of direct government grant there has been little reason for UGC funds to be committed to it; but the grant regulations specify 'the liberal education of adults' as the sole area for which grant may be paid. What does this mean in relation to the new sophisticated publics requiring post-experience study in applied science, or advanced work in social administration, or post-graduate medical education? In practice the DES have been remarkably generous in their interpretation of this rubric, but quite rightly it cannot be set aside. A good deal of ingenuity has had to go into devising forms of words that will save the regulations' face, or into raising funds elsewhere; and the paradoxical situation has arisen that it has become easier for a university extra-mural department to develop the traditional work of which the determinants lie outside the university, than the New Extension work which is a direct outflow of the university itself.

It has also to be recognized that some universities have been uncommonly generous towards their work in adult education and have made UGC funds available to it on an increasing scale. For example the lead given by Leicester in establishing teaching centres for university adult education, first at Vaughan College and then at Northampton, has been followed by a number of other universities, in recognition of the need to provide intra-mural conditions of study for those who cannot reach the main campus. The result is that, of the £2·5 million or so spent annually on university adult education in England and Wales, much less than half comes from DES grant; and if a realistic costing of central services was done, the proportion borne by the DES would be no more than about one-third. Yet the impression persists that the DES meets 75 per cent of the cost. (What the regulations say is that the DES may pay *up to 75 per cent* of the teaching costs; and these are very narrowly defined.) The truth is that a relatively small grant from central government funds has made potentially available to local communities the resources of knowledge of the entire university world: which is not a bad bargain, and it is the extra-mural departments' own momentum, by and large, that has brought it about.

To say this is not to be complacent either about the present or about the future. Change is now normal in the universities, in the whole field of higher education and in society at large. Adult education is now a much wider world than the classes of the extra-mural departments and the WEA. The major providers in formal terms are now the local education authorities, some of which have well-developed services of adult education with professional staff and appropriate premises. The agencies that bring systematic learning opportunities to the greatest number of adults are the broadcasting services through their further and adult education output. The Open University has built on these to offer a specifically undergraduate level of teaching, with the promise of post-graduate work to follow soon. Moreover, although as teaching institutions the universities are now absolutely bigger than formerly (and therefore have larger teaching resources) they are relatively smaller within the higher education options of the school leaver. As research institutions they no longer have the virtual monopoly they once enjoyed but must relate to a wide spectrum of establishments funded by government, industry, private trusts and commercial enterprise. As universities have grown their range of specialisms has widened, embracing fresh areas of teaching but also refining and sharpening the sub-divisions within subjects; and the greater size of universities has meant that the units with which, for academic purposes, the teaching staff tend to identify are the departments and schools rather than their university as a whole. Improved travel has strengthened the links in international networks of scholarship but may have weakened cross-disciplinary links within the university or between the university and the locality. Each of these changes, clearly visible already, must be regarded as a trend for the future too. So the question is whether, in the context of these changes, there is a role in adult education that is still unique to the universities and that could not be handed over to other institutions. Would not the whole job be better left to the LEAs, the broadcasters, the Open University, the polytechnics and the rest, while the universities grapple with their own problems of growth and priorities? Ironically, it is through the very nature of these problems of growth and priority that this question demands an answer. The universities cannot get out of it quite so easily.

V

We speak of universities as institutions of learning, as though learning was a product or commodity. (We even speak in the same vein—or more commonly are spoken to—about our productivity.) Learning does not occur in institutions but in individuals. It is a process that goes on, with greater or less discouragement, through-out any person's life; and because of the continuity of the person, each stage of learning affects and is affected by each other stage—including the undergraduate. It is all too easy to think of the collective student body as springing fully armed from the head of an A-level pass list, pursuing a sort of half-life for three years, and then being passed, graded and stamped like eggs, into a store called graduate manpower. It is much harder to see the students as people at a particular (and variable) stage of development, coming in to us for a brief period from a continuous life else-where, their attitudes to learning and expectations of its nature and value already largely formed; to remember that those attitudes and expectations will have been influenced by their teachers, who are an earlier, not to say archaic, generation of students, and also by many of those common men who have seen only the outside walls of a university; to acknowledge that three years (some would say, three years on half-time) are not much in which to re-formu-late attitudes, but that the attitudes and expectations with which our graduates leave are those of the teachers and many of the common man's opinion-leaders for the next forty years or so—unless something is done about them. The whole concept of a 'degree', a fixed step of pre-ordained height affording a permanent vantage-point, belongs to a static universe. But universities are committed to a dynamic view of knowledge, as something con-stantly being enlarged, redefined and revalued. To work as hard as universities do to render obsolete the seals of approval they have themselves awarded is to treat their graduates scurvily and to give society a poor return for the great sums spent on them.

This involves much more than is commonly understood by 'up-dating'. Knowledge is more than know-how. The universities as centres of intellectual excellence will not be primarily concerned with economic yields, with adding to the sum of material goods and services, though their research may have this effect. Nor will they be directly concerned with the solving of problems. Their field is to assemble structures of knowledge, to formulate theories and to test them objectively, to stand firm on the truthful and clear communication of ideas, to think out the long perspectives in terms of the quality of life. Up-dating implies the adding of further layers to a fixed foundation: universities ought to be questioning the foundation too, and showing the possibility of alternative foundations. But it may all be rather beautifully pointless unless these values of university study are communicated to those who do have to produce solutions, for the quality of life depends also on society's ability to solve its problems.

We are close here to the currently fashionable European concept of *éducation permanente*, which is an attempt to visualize education as a continuing thread of experiences in the life-span of the individual, and to replace the idea of educational provision as a sequence of institutions for given age-ranges with the idea of a set of options permanently open, including the option of recourse to universities at whatever stage of life is appropriate. The factors that may make such recourse appropriate are many and varied. They will include prior academic attainment, as in post-graduate courses; but they will also include experience of other kinds, either in a role in society or in some other educational milieu, or simply in a sense of disadvantage and a determination to repair it.

VI

It then becomes possible to envisage certain principles for a university's 'adult education' that may be expected to hold good whatever the directions of change in universities. In the first place, if undergraduate teaching is conceived of as the first instalment of an educational continuum, then opportunities for return at intervals will be needed. These will include the present kinds of post-graduate, in-service and post-experience work, but also much more substantial periods of study, perhaps attached to research or project groups or as members of ongoing seminars. The university will need to be *open* in the fullest sense to its own members.

Secondly, universities as parts of the total education system will need to contribute to the continued working of the system their unique resources as institutions of rigorous and high-level study. The Robbins principle of open access for all who show ability to benefit from a university represents simple justice if equality of educational opportunity remains one of the goals of our society; it just happens to be impossibly costly if applied to school-leavers, with the expenses of full-time study, maintenance grants and so on. But it is not unattainable in the terms in which access to university study is being considered here. Not everyone wants a full degree course. Patterns of employment are changing in ways that break down the old distinctions of full-time day and part-time evening study. There is already enough accumulated experience in their extra-mural work to show that universities can transmit their values in part-time courses of limited duration.

Thirdly, however, the converse follows, that those who discover in mature life the need for a degree or other university qualification should be enabled to plan and pursue their studies in a structure that will lead to graduation. This will raise difficult questions of transferability between courses and institutions and mutual acceptance of component courses of study. It is inconceivable that such questions should prove insoluble if there is any true meaning in university standards.

Fourthly, universities will need to be more explicit about what their standards are, if the precise needs of the public are to be met. At present one suspects that many young people are railroaded forward into universities by a system that never requires them to ask or to discover why they are there. For all the changes of attitude in the general public there is still a mystique about universities, as anyone who has had to interview applicants for mature scholarships will know. If indeed universities are to be open in the way I have been suggesting, there must be access to an advice and information service through which the purposes and the true demands of university study can be made clear.

At this point one is concerned with machinery as well as with principles and the question arises whether a specific department, such as an extra-mural department, is needed. This is probably something which each university would want to consider in its own situation. Several new universities with an interest in adult education have so far not set up traditional departments, and several of the existing departments have been radically restructured after careful review. There is no one right pattern. But certain functions are inescapable: the identification and locating of publics for specific kinds of study; the advisory function; co-ordination and consultation with outside bodies, including the rest of the education service; and above all, research and evaluation. These are all tasks which are already being carried out by the existing departments to a greater or less degree, and it would seem to make for simplicity if they are grouped into one unit. What is quite essential is that the old concept of an 'extra-mural' department, operating beyond walls which conceal the true life of the university, should be abandoned and the opening of the full resources of the university to the larger community should take its place.

Rediscovering identity in higher education

W. A. C. Stewart

Vice-Chancellor of the University of Keele

H

When Robbins reported in 1963 he made the point that there have been Royal Commissions on particular universities, committees on technical education and on the training of teachers, but never a committee on the pattern of higher education in Great Britain. It would be a misnomer to speak of a 'system' of higher education in this country. Technical, commercial, art and training colleges (to use the old titles) have grown up separately and universities, more or less independent of the state and in many ways of the school system, have dominated the landscape.

The Robbins proposals are based on the assumption that there now must be a system operating with co-ordinating principles. For Robbins, only eight or nine years ago, working to his terms of reference and reviewing 'the pattern of full-time higher education', only universities and training colleges formed that sector. He included also a section on further education and this incorporated Colleges of Advanced Technology (which have since entered the higher education grouping and have become universities), Regional Colleges, Area Colleges, Local Colleges and Colleges of Art and Commerce. It is reasonable to see the growth of education as a whole and higher education in particular as being unco-ordinated in the past century and a half. First of all, schoooling changes from being the prerogative of minorities of one kind or another, to broader and broader applicability. The extended principle is formulated as a drive for universal literacy, and then as provision for compulsory schooling between certain ages, and later still as the need to meet the democratic right of every individual to compulsory general education.

If we turn from the broad base of compulsory general education we also find the accompanying transformations in specialized and advanced education. Social and economic historians, with or without Marxist tools, have shown how and why the availability of university education in Britain broadened out from an aristocracy of birth to one of worth through new civic university foundations, in the industrialized wealth of the nineteenth century. A narrower focus, to which words like 'vocation' and 'training', rather than 'education', became attached, produced nineteenth- and twentieth-century changes in art, commercial, industrial and technical provision and in the training colleges. Now we have shifted the focus from historical and unco-ordinated provision for vocational training to political and social emphasis on equality of educational opportunity and to education according to individual ability and aptitude.

II

If the Open University is included, there are forty-five universities in Britain. Of these, ten were Colleges of Advanced Technology which became universities in 1964 and 1965. Besides these forty-five, the College of Aeronautics at Cranfield became the Cranfield Institute of Technology by Royal Charter in 1969 and prepares for higher degrees and postgraduate courses only. The Royal College of Art was given a Royal Charter in 1967 and it too does not enrol students for first degrees. Here we begin to get into the fine print of higher administration. Forty-four universities receive their major finance and administer their policy through the University Grants Committee. The Open University, Cranfield, and the RCA are administered direct from the Department of Education and Science. Until 1964 universities had a special line through the UGC direct to the Treasury for their claim on the educational budget. Since 1964 the UGC is responsible to the Department of Education and Science and it is for the Secretary of State to balance the claims of universities, schools and other branches of education. Universities and the UGC are no longer the unique and separated aristocracy.

For clarification (and we shall need it) and in summary there are forty-four universities instituted by Royal Charter and responsible to the University Grants Committee. There are three university-type institutions, Cranfield, the Royal College of Art and the Open University (the first two of them for postgraduate work only, the third for both undergraduate and postgraduate work), also instituted by Royal Charter and responsible direct to the government Department of Education and Science. No new universities are to be created in Britain in the next nine or ten years.

Before 1963 the institutions in England and Wales which prepared teachers were called training colleges. Since the Robbins Report they have been called colleges of education and the broader horizons implied in the change of name are obvious. Since 1946 the colleges in England and Wales (Scotland and Ireland are different) have been associated with Area Training Organizations, all but one of which (Cambridge was and still is the exception) are linked into university government and organization through the University Institutes of Education. Besides monitoring and approving academic courses for the Certificate of Education, the universities validate the award and from 1968 onwards have also been awarding the Bachelor of Education degree to selected students undertaking a fourth year. The training of teachers has therefore been a direct and indirect university responsibility since 1946 and the colleges of education were seen by Robbins as part of higher education. There are over 160 colleges, about one-third of them voluntary colleges, mainly religious foundations, and the rest are responsible to local authorities. Where universities look to the UGC in financial and academic matters, the colleges of education look to the Department of Education and Science, to their LEAs or voluntary governors, and only academically speaking to the universities.

In May 1966 a White Paper indicated that a new type of institution called a *polytechnic* would be established and this would probably be in the higher education sector at some point, but would not be a university. It is the most difficult thing in the world to found such an educational institution, define its principles and purposes and place it definitively within the British educational provision, especially in the higher and further sectors of education. But why found polytechnics at all? Partly because there was (and is) a very considerable proportion of degree or near-degree level work being done in a variety of further education establishments. Partly because the Robbins detonations created expectations of floods of students who could not be accommodated even in greatly expanded universities. Partly because if colleges of education were to be allied with universities administratively, financially and academically, the former area colleges and regional colleges of art, commerce and technology would be likely to aspire in the same direction. Partly because a non-university body awarding degrees and diplomas was set up by Royal Charter in 1964. This was the Council for National Academic Awards and it has the power to award degrees and diplomas of any kind based upon central approval of courses framed by the colleges.

In one sense the founding of polytechnics was an attempt to rationalize an area of part-time and full-time education in the further education sector, and to move the polytechnics into the bracket of higher education where the colleges of education already were with the universities. In another sense the creation of polytechnics was an act of containment on two sides—on the one hand towards the universities from which, according to nearly everyone, they differed; on the other hand towards the other colleges of further education into which the lower level work would be directed from the polytechnics. It would be best to summarize the main features of the polytechnics as the 1966 White Paper saw them.

They were to be high-level institutions, 'the main centres of full-time higher education within the Further Education system'. However, they were to retain a 'comprehensive' function in that they could provide for sub-degree work which earned a high-level national diploma and for this the students could attend full-time or part-time. They were not to be new custom-built institutions, but existing colleges up-graded and extended and where necessary two or more neighbouring institutions could be linked under one governing body to form a single academic foundation. A college of art, a college of commerce, a college of technology, could form the new amalgamation. In Leeds and Liverpool four colleges have to be associated and in Birmingham five. Sometimes the various units are miles apart, with the attendant problems of identity and policy. As a former Minister of State for Education, Mr Gerald Fowler, said in a speech in 1969:

> To a few—very few—designation means little more than changing the brass plate at the college entrance. . . . At the other end of the scale designation is little more than an act of faith.

As all the colleges already had an identity and life in the further education structure, the first problem has been one of de-identification and re-assembly.

About 70 per cent of all full-time and sandwich course students are in the thirty polytechnics, the other 30 per cent being in about seventy other colleges. The non-advanced courses in the polytechnics have dropped by 40 per cent in five years and only 20 per cent of them are now to be found in polytechnics. About 98 per cent of the 288 courses approved by the CNAA in 1970–1 are to be found in polytechnics together with 80 per cent of the external degree of work of the University of London. Courses like those for the Higher National Diploma are fairly evenly split between polytechnics and other Colleges of Further Education. These trends towards locating advanced work in polytechnics, while keeping some features of a 'comprehensive' institution, have produced wide variations in these early years of transition. In five polytechnics taken as a sample in 1970 the proportion of degree work varied from 24 per cent in one to 81 per cent in another with two between 40 and 49 per cent and one just over 70 per cent. In 1969–70 there were 639 CNAA students reading for Masters' degrees and doctorates in polytechnics as compared with about 20,000 taking first degrees, which is slightly over 3 per cent. The percentage of research students in universities is about 18 per cent of the 220,000 enrolled.[1]

Let me try to take a few bearings amid these very rough statistics. Polytechnics are edging into the higher education bracket while at present being located in 'advanced further education'. They have a concentration of full-time and sandwich advanced courses but still maintain a 'comprehensive' spread of part-time day and evening advanced courses. The number of advanced day courses is pretty considerable and has grown over the period 1966–70 by 22 per cent while the evening advanced courses have dwindled by 3 per cent over the same period. During this period the non-advanced courses diminished by nearly 40 per cent in the polytechnics. In all, the polytechnic courses, whether full-time or part-time, day or evening, incorporate 70 per cent of the advanced work in further education.

So far the amount and proportion of research and higher degree work done in polytechnics does not, and is not intended to, compare with what is done in universities. However, I believe that in taught courses for Masters' degrees, especially in the humanities and social sciences, the number and proportion of degrees will increase considerably, but probably will not, in the near future at least, challenge the predominance of the university.

The total number of students taking degrees in 1970 through CNAA and the University of London external programme was about 31,000 (divided 20,000 and 11,000) which is roughly double what it was in 1964 when CNAA was established. Of these 31,000 some 28,000 were in polytechnics. We should see this in a perspective of just under 160,000 in all kinds of Further Education colleges on all kinds of course and it represents about 17 per cent. If we turn to Colleges of Education in England and Wales at the same point we find about 110,000 students in various full-time courses, of which about 10 per cent, on a rising gradient since 1968, took Bachelor of Education degrees over the four-year full-time course. Polytechnics regard themselves as being at least as deserving as Colleges of Education of being in the higher education bracket.

For Colleges of Education the pattern is the life of a full-time student and this corresponds to the position for the huge majority of university students. Technological universities and polytechnics have a heritage of part-time study either from day-release or evening work which is different from the prevailing full-time university pattern. The recent variation introduced by the sandwich course in the university and the polytechnic has a base of full-time study in the parent institution with a layer of full-time practical work made more systematically a part of the whole course than is the case with the earlier type of university student of engineering or medicine, who appeared in his practical work to resemble an apprentice-student out on licence from his professor. The polytechnic student in industrial experience is seen while he is there as involved more completely in the business. All this is changing, of course, as business schools in universities and polytechnics overlap and the technological universities bring the value of practical experience more massively into the non-vocational university spectrum.

III

Universities have been and still are at the peak of the educational pyramid. They are there for social reasons, now much less potent, stemming from 800 years of Oxford and Cambridge and 500 years of St Andrews, Glasgow, Aberdeen and Edinburgh. I am not disposed to belittle the real value of that social inheritance. Of course it has had its ridiculous snobberies and pathetic posturings; but it has given generations of students and dons a style of living and growing with ideas (different maybe between Scotland and England) which the great majority never wholly forget. And snobberies and posturings can be found at Westminster, in the Trades Unions and in local government.

More important than the social advantages, it is the intellectual expectations that place the universities at the peak of the educational pyramid. The selection and teaching of able young people at undergraduate level, and the responsibility for advanced study and research resting on the staff, combine to make a university a very special place. A day or two at Edinburgh, Hull, Durham, Manchester, Keele, Nottingham, Cambridge, London, Exeter, Brunel and Kent would establish the institutional differences between these universities; but each has its own confidence in being a university. If this is regarded as a facile and arrogant generality, let me suggest a simple test. What would be the effect of a proposal to take away the title of 'university' from any one of the forty-five? Indeed, who would or could make such a proposal and on what grounds? The loss of confidence both inside the university and outside it before such a thing could be contemplated would have to be immense.

After the sociologists have examined the structure and function of the institution; the class stratification of the educational system with special reference to the upward social mobility of the graduate; the differential economic advantage of the degree as an index of social privilege—when these have been examined, with all the questions begged that the formulations of the problems indicate, the universities will still be at the peak of the educational pyramid. A very powerful part of their confidence in that position has to do with a mystique compounded, first, of the Oxbridge-Scottish heritage; second, of the recognition that universities are places where by and large the ablest people intellectually will work and be taught; third, of the British technique of insulating the university from local government and national government political swings, of which the constitution and function of the University Grants Committee before 1964 was an example. Added to these features has been the infusion of civic pride which led to the foundation of local or regional universities originally focused upon the neighbourhood need but now purged by experience to recognize, whether at Leeds or Sussex, that a university will not blossom unless it is national and international in its appeal. For such reasons the proposed Independent University hopes to have Fellows of the Royal Society and of the British Academy among its founder professors to establish its credentials in the academic commonwealth.

Mystique is all very well but administration, economics, the politics of equality of opportunity, man-power planning, cost-effectiveness, the expansion of tertiary, not to mention quaternary, education—all these make the future prospect of the university very different from the past and the position at the peak of the pyramid far more open to challenge than ever before. There is a much stronger tendency to ask what a university does and why it does it, to see the university as part of a social, economic and institutional structure. Indeed, this functional approach has provided one of the main reasons why some students and teachers are searching anew for the personal and educational dimensions of higher education—for what are variously called more personalized, problem-oriented, open-ended curricula or whatever the hurrah words may be.

IV

The main participants in the central administration of higher education are the government of the day (mainly through its Department of Education and Science); the University Grants Committee; the Committee of Vice-Chancellors and Principals; the professional associations of teachers and students (whether the Association of University Teachers, the Association of Teachers in Technical Institutions, the Association of Teachers in Colleges and Departments of Education, the National Union of Students, or others); and the federation of Local Authority Associations.

The UGC is made up of a growing permanent secretariat and a policy-forming committee of just over twenty people, three-fifths of whom are full-time university persons. They also have seventeen expert sub-committees dealing with academic disciplines. It used to be said that the UGC operated on the 'buffer principle', offering a communication link between the universities, the Treasury and the government. In 1967 the then Chairman said that the UGC was not now so much a buffer as the 'designer of a general strategic pattern' for producing scarce and highly skilled man-power. This exercise had to be carried out economically and efficiently and with a due regard to university autonomy, and increasingly the responsibility on the UGC and the universities for the effective use of scarce national resources has been emphasized.[2] What has happened is that the communicating link offered by the UGC remains, but the Committee's role in relation to each individual university is now much more decisive. The small secretariat has become a much larger and expert staff of over 120, sophisticated in costing, in building, in statistical forecasting. The UGC in its *Memorandum of General Guidance*, first produced in 1967 and now a continuing feature, indicates where large-scale decisions have been made—that 320,000 students in universities by 1977 is their working hypothesis; that 45 per cent of these should be arts based and 55 per cent science based; that 18 per cent of the total should be postgraduates; that between 1972 and 1977 there should be no new schools of architecture in universities; that specialist concentrations in educational technology should be located in certain places; that certain limits of numbers of students have been placed on each university to arrive at these general policy conclusions. The trend in all this is that a strategy for universities is being devised 'fully adequate to national needs' and the particular outcome is that the UGC will increasingly be saying to university X either implicitly or explicitly, 'Do not expand architecture: enlarge the medical school to an annual intake of 100: there will be no money to maintain the uneconomic department of Y.' In other words the co-ordinating and planning role of the central organization is likely to increase and the independent planning of individual universities will decrease. The block grant for five years, which is the present basis of UGC allocation, is made on the basis of forecasts and proposals from the universities and there is as little earmarking or 'indicating' of sectional approvals as possible—it is a block grant which the university has to allocate in detail. However, the dilemma of increased central planning and formula-costing inevitably will make 'indications' appear like instructions; and this dilemma must be accepted as a fact of future life.

The UGC itself is exposed to increasing pressures from the government, from parliament, Treasury, the Department of Education and Science, or elsewhere. It has to await from the government a declaration on such vital matters as the following: the amount of capital available for university building from 1973 onward; the number of university students the government will be prepared to support during 1972–7 (and this figure the government need not divulge until June 1972, with the new quinquennium beginning in October); the attitude to the James Committee's report on the training of teachers, the Committee having been given only one year by the government in which to examine the whole problem and being due to report early in 1972. The pressure of parliament can be no less severe. The Select Committee on Education and Science produced a Report on *Student Relations* in which the UGC was accused of interpreting its terms of reference too narrowly; giving little attention to the social effects of expansion; allowing a haphazard proliferation of courses in universities; and failing to investigate the significance of staff/student ratios.[3] The Public Accounts Committee in the Session 1969–70 reviewed for the first time matters affecting the UGC, the DES and certain universities arising out of the first report of the Comptroller and Auditor General on the session 1968–9.[4] Undoubtedly the UGC witnesses were submitted to an aggressive cross-examination.

These pressures are likely to increase rather than decrease and it will be more and more difficult to uphold the Robbins principle: '[the UGC is] a committee independent of politics and not subject to ministerial direction, yet maintaining close contact with the organization of Government, which advises the Chancellor on the magnitude of the amounts needed and distributes the funds made available'. That was written in 1963 before the UGC was brought into the DES organization instead of having direct access to the Treasury, and before the Comptroller and Auditor General and the Committee of Public Accounts had direct access to the books of the UGC and individual universities. The Robbins Report directly opposed these changes in advance and a reasonable case can be made out to show that the remaining independence of the UGC is being attacked in the interest of cutting the universities down to size, lowering their status so that the standing of other educational institutions may be built up.

The binary system has produced polytechnics, as we have seen, which have a very considerable degree level output through CNAA. They seek an increasing amount of university-type governance—academic boards; boards of governors on which teaching staff, besides the Director, are represented; a decentralization of authority, and a large increase in democratic government. Included in this is student participation, and it will be only a matter of time before polytechnics will seek to be known as universities. The CNAA approval for degrees is usually given for a period of five years, after which the scrutiny is repeated. Within the next decade the more powerful polytechnics, at least, are almost certain to seek to award their own degrees, and of course the present position of the Cranfield Institute of Technology and the Royal College of Art offer enticing precedents.

If some polytechnics become degree-granting institutions outside the UGC system, how many would there need to be before the demand for a separate or more comprehensive Grants Committee became imperative? There has been a proposal for a separate Local Authority Higher Education Committee and another for a Technology Grants Committee on the UGC pattern, each advocating different solutions for the co-ordination of polytechnics. Mr Eric Robinson wants to widen tertiary education policy so that colleges of education and polytechnics should stop aspiring to university links and status and should align with further education and adult education. In these terms Mr Robinson thinks that the universities should abandon the position of being 'a self-justifying, intrinsically good, seeker after truth' and should accept 'a social role requiring instrumental justification both in gross and in detail'.[5] The Parliamentary Select Committee recommended absorbing the UGC into a comprehensive Higher Education Commission which would apparently have consultative, advisory and financial responsibilities. The Committee deplores the division of higher education into universities and non-university institutions and ascribes the basic cause of the division to the different ways in which they are financed.[6]

During the seventies one recurring theme is therefore going to be the identity of the university. It is at present an institution concerned with high quality learning, whether for undergraduates or postgraduates. It operates through selection and competitive criteria for entry. The autonomy of each university is based on the mysterious but hitherto respected status of a Royal Charter and Statutes, and the policy of administration has been different from that of any other educational institution in that the universities through the UGC have a protection of their own from direct contact and possible conflict with government and political power either local or national.

There will be persons and forces in society tending sharply for and against the pre-eminent position of the university. Those who see the university as having a social role emphasize two main features: first, the 'needs of society', especially high-level man-power needs, and the role of the university here is to train the experts and upper-level professionals; second, concern for the university as part of a whole system of education stretching from primary to tertiary. The main consequence of both these features is uncompromising emphasis on the present and the future, on the organizational and functional. The idea of the scholarly tradition, the austerity as well as the advantages in the university, is questioned or disregarded. The emphasis of the academics, on the other hand, is to look at knowledge and its *bona fides*, to see the institution as being mainly concerned with good and often difficult study. For them, even if the study is socially useful, its validation is in the personal integrity of the student and the cumulative effect study has on his ethical and intellectual development; for this is seen as the justification of scholarly endeavour, whether conducted in a university or in a primary school.

The academic concern tends to be exclusive rather than inclusive in its social thinking, and the reverse is true of the sociological concern. Each viewpoint incorporates an implicit view of the university and the functions it ought to discharge as one of society's institutions. During the seventies the social emphasis is going to gain in power because the economic and political dimensions are paramount in educational planning. In order to maintain any sense of continuity with the university tradition, academics will need increasingly to understand how to navigate the currents in planning. If in the past the UGC has been a buffer which has protected academics and the universities, the Public Accounts Committee, the Parliamentary Select Committee and the new policies recommended by Lord Rothschild's committee consider-ing the future of government research have shown that the UGC is going to be under fire in future as never before.

The proud old slogan of individual autonomy for universities is now much modified as they have recognized the inevitability and the justice of planning and co-ordination. Yet the principle of autonomy is a good one if it is understood as an attempt to ensure some freedom of choice. But the dilemmas remain for the individual university and might be stated thus—how much to be free to choose and decide for itself, how much to declare common interest with other universities, either regionally or nationally, to challenge the UGC; how much to identify 'a university interest' in common with the UGC to challenge the government or the Local Authorities; how much to separate from other sectors of education in the interests of defending university essentials; how much to join with other sectors of higher and further education to seek educational justice. Yet when the problems have been identified, it is not a matter only of principle but of practice, not a matter of how much but simply of how? How can autonomous universities discover and articulate the collective opinion which will be supremely necessary in the seventies?

The body through which this may most obviously be done is the Committee of Vice-Chancellors and Principals. This body now has expressed opinion on behalf of university interests in topical and critical affairs such as the totally unexpected increase by the government in 1966 of overseas students' fees, or student order and discipline in 1968 and 1969, or the proposals of the Prices and Incomes Board on increases in university salaries. Obviously on policy matters the CVCP speaks to the UGC and sometimes direct to Ministers—for instance, on increase in the numbers of students in a quinquennium; on university entrance standards and the setting up of the Universities Central Council for Admissions. The CVCP operates with the UGC, the AUT and the DES on salary matters, following a dissatisfaction with the working of the Prices and Incomes Board: the Committee represents the university interest on the body dealing with clerical, technical and manual staffs employed by universities. The CVCP also produces reports and initiates conferences on matters of general interest—the annual *Compendium of University Entrance Requirements*, the *Report on the Quinquennium 1962–67*, *University Development in the Seventies*: conferences on examination and assessment, university residence, committee structure in higher education. With all the concern for autonomy, universities can see that there is urgent need for joint negotiation and a joint voice. In the next decade the confidence in, and the confidence of, the CVCP must increase if there is to be some kind of university case in the arguments which lie ahead. Yet it must respect the right of the individual university. This dilemma is one which the Committee itself has to face every time new decisions have to be made. Should *all* universities accept a collective decision on student membership of Senates and Councils? Should *all* universities agree to participate in providing individualized data, with proper safeguards for confidentiality? What are proper safeguards? Should the CVCP respond collectively to the thirteen proposals from the DES on economy measures or should universities do so individually? In what sense did the CVCP speak for universities in the joint statement with the National Union of Students in 1968 on student discipline in a time of unrest? The CVCP will in its fashion increasingly come to articulate the centralizing tendency which the UGC has had correspondingly to articulate in its sphere of influence.

This dilemma of a central organization which might or might not speak for individual bodies is repeated wherever any sector of a university's interests is concerned. The National Union of Students over the last six or seven years has been walking on hot coals in this matter. The Council and Executive, the mandated representatives at conferences, the student members in individual universities, the large body of uninterested students—these all can represent conflicting views when concerted opinion is being sought, let alone co-ordinated action being agreed upon and taken. *Mutatis mutandis*, the same holds for the position of the Association of University Teachers, the professional trade union of academics. Their position is being challenged (so far with limited success) by the more militant organization of the Association of Scientific Technical and Managerial Staffs, to which some academics, administrators, technicians and scientists already belong. The AUT now has a recognized place in salary negotiations at the national level and is seeking recognition as a negotiating body in individual universities, which in most cases renders formal what has been the case for many years. The traditional areas of negotiating wages and conditions of work are only part of what the AUT is after.

It could happen that in the seventies, as universities and other parts of tertiary education are expected to work more closely together, salary differentials, conditions of work in terms or vacations, leave of absence, time accountability, and authority structure, will come into the arena of argument and acrimony as one or other of the trade unions now edging into the universities joins issue in particular places. It is significant that the AUT has in July 1971 declared that it will not affiliate with the Trades Union Congress to which the ASTMS and the Association of

Teachers in Technical Institutions are attached. The university trades unions will have to interpret anew in the seventies what university autonomy as compared with central organization really amounts to and what belonging to a profession means.

One of the clear lessons from the student unrest of 1968 onwards, less in Britain than on the Continent, but clear enough here, was the attempt to politicize everything—to declare 'sides', to negotiate, to produce mandates, to confront, to make Students Unions either trade unions or radical political parties. In universities this startled academics, administrators and students alike, for rightly or wrongly this was not the British university style at all. Much ground has been traversed in these three years and the deep issues of authority structure, the social and intellectual authorization of the university, have been uncovered. Most of the talk about representation has to do with accommodating the conflicts to see if some new agreed assumptions of tolerance and mutual acceptance can be lastingly worked out. The seventies is a time when the authority of the academic subject, of the teacher and of the institution has to be rewritten in acceptance by the student and the teacher of one another. The confrontation style is based on conflict and acceptance of function only. The best of the university style has to do with relations of persons with mutually compatible skills, even in the context of intellectual abrasion. The tests of the seventies will be to see if politics and economics are more powerful determinants of university life than a revised version of the university style which must incorporate the need for political and economic revaluations of higher education and its purposes and methods in a more profound understanding between people.

v

The promise of over 800,000 in tertiary education by the early eighties with a school-leaving age of sixteen from 1973 raises questions of the reliability of such forecasts. I do not propose to enter that kind of discussion. It is sufficient for my purpose that the present figures in higher education are likely to double yet again in ten years. This faces successive governments with enormous difficulties of which I will mention only two. A build-up of this size demands a strategy over a period of years, and govern-

I

ments are unwilling to commit their successors; but if this task is to be brought off they have to. The second difficulty is the 'educated society', 'national need', 'me too' principle—whatever one calls it—by which education is seen as an unlimited good which ought only to increase. The difficulty is to foresee how to pay for it, or, to put it another way, how to place a limit which can be justifiably defended aside from the principle 'This, being all we can afford, is the best we can do'. This is, after all, the principle which guides us now; but the new feature is that for many people, more institutionally supplied education means 'better always and all the time'. This is not intended as a disguised version of 'more will mean worse'. What I have in mind is 'When will more come to mean that we have no money to pay for it?' Higher education is well known as the most expensive sector and in the seventies I see an increased attention being given to value for money in higher education—not in a mean-minded sense, but in a desire to spread provision as widely as possible and so trying to find economical and unorthodox methods.

The dangers of shortening courses are already known and there is a strong resistance to reducing still further an obviously short university or college course. However, some people will try to support a three-year degree course for teachers, when at present the course is for four years. The move will be urged to provide two-year courses as the first part of a two-part qualification which can be completed at either stage with an appropriate award. We are told that the James Committee has this in mind.

While the governors of polytechnics and colleges of education try to provide social and residential amenities for their students comparable with those which many universities have had, universities climbing up to 10,000 and more are finding residential places for students increasingly hard to get. The capital cost of housing students is going to mount more steeply than ever, even with self-help arrangements and co-operative ventures in large cities. In any case, housing conditions are going to affect radically the kind of universities we have in future. A collegiate institution like Oxbridge or Kent or York is different from Glasgow or Aberdeen with their high percentage of local-born students living at home and using a Union building. Each of them is different again from Manchester with a large precinct in which UGC and loan-financed residences are going to house students from the university and the binary colleges, and the informal living arrangements will help to influence the nature of the contrast between the colleges and the university.

Behind the problems of residence lies the likelihood of recommending that more students should live at home, thus stressing the regional importance of the university rather than its national and international significance. Is a regional plan politically possible in a youth culture like ours? Is it possible or fair when academic choices point to another university? Will the binary colleges take to this regional style more easily than the universities? These questions arise inexorably out of thinking how to pay for the higher education of 800,000 students in ten years' time.

So too does the issue of full-time and part-time education. The universities believe mostly in full-time studies, but technical education has the tradition of day-release or evening studies, with the correspondingly more intensive use of 'plant' and larger numbers of students, even if each one takes longer. The university and the college of education have always laid much store by the personal benefits of all kinds to be obtained from the informal community life. I believe this is still quite strongly supported, but it is in conflict with another and newer attitude. Some students do not want to be identified with this kind of 'university culture', believing that this isolates them from the society they wish to serve and reform. This conviction may take the form of wanting to be accepted by 'the workers' or merging the university with all those other institutions which are held to need radical change. In either case the student does not want to be in a bourgeois, privileged and politically ineffectual occupation. For him 'the university community' is a device to neutralize the political effectiveness of the student body, diverting them from full membership of society. Living in lodgings suits him better.

With all the concern for economy and the full use of 'plant', such experiments as have been tried with the four-term year or its variants[7] have not been really acceptable; and when all the objections have been summarized one of the most weighty has been that the educational and social community has been disrupted, both for students and staff. Will this continue to be a relevant argument when the majority of universities are over 6,000 strong? Will social justice and economic pressure in ten years' time lead to a re-statement of educational objectives?

VI

Let me attempt to gather together the threads from these reflections. Through all that has been said in this essay the central problem is one of identity. What will be the assumed marks of *the university* in the seventies and the eighties? Will it be a recognizable term used for a specific institution? Will the polyversity or the multiversity in fact replace the university? Even if the name persists, will the institution be recognizably similar to the one we know now?

In Great Britain the university now operates through selection and competitive entry. It teaches both undergraduates and graduates and pursues research. Its systems of internal government have rested and still rest on the authority of the teaching staff whether through the democracy of Fellows in the Oxbridge colleges or the more oligarchic organization of a Senate and its committees in the civic universities. Redbrick also has the joint lay and academic government of a Council dealing with non-academic matters. Only universities have this degree of participation together with academic and administrative freedom. I believe that universities will seek to preserve this at all costs in the future. It is very likely that polytechnics and colleges of education will do all they can to adopt these modes of internal government in the next decade. Obviously, any proposal to set up a 'multiversity' organization will have at once to come to terms with the different modes of internal organization in universities and colleges. The changes taking place in government in the maintained sector of further and higher education tend towards the university style, but in the majority of cases have still some distance to go. This situation recurs *mutatis mutandis* in the government of student unions.

Academically, as we have seen, there is already a good proportion of degree level work being done in polytechnics and an increasing amount in colleges of education; and the overlap with universities is considerable although there is also a variety of advanced non-degree work in the binary sector which is likely to remain.

The means of financing the various institutions are different, but there may well be pressure to bring them together, to merge the UGC into some larger national or possibly regional organization in order to bring about a national administration of higher education, both in policy and finance. In such an arrangement universities would be one of a number of partners dealt with on relatively equal terms nationally and probably regionally as well. But what of the intellectual, moral and academic aspects *within* each university, and its view of its own role to its students?

Universities in the seventies and eighties of this century have to be aware of what they are teaching and why, with a new clarity. New universities have had to face this issue and arrive at a definition of content and method. More broadly they have had to define a *university* pattern which can be both commended and defended. Keele and the newer universities are concerned about general and specific education. Sussex and Essex and East Anglia are planned on the basis of Schools of Study rather than on departments. London and Durham and Birmingham and Leeds had to think as *universities* many years ago when they first had freedom and independence. Now the massive organization based on departments, faculties, degree structures, buildings, hardware, not to mention personal commitment, makes it virtually impossible for these large, established universities to produce a new *university* plan even if they wanted to. New combinations of subjects can be produced, new departments or institutes can be added, new curricula devised, but if the university is to retain coherence these have to be administered within a framework capable of admitting a plurality of programmes and operating a whole variety of subsystems. The new universities have some years to go before they find themselves in such a case, for they are still based on a general and known degree pattern.

The point to make here, however, is that in future universities will have to be explicit about what they offer. Let me take two examples. The University of Birmingham offers degrees at honours or pass levels; a spread of subjects ranging through several faculties and a very large number of departments; courses lasting three, four, five or six years for the first qualification; postgraduate degrees based on research and theses and others based on further study and examinations; research departments which produce, not necessarily for higher degrees, original results whether 'applied' or not; resources in music and fine art and drama which relate to the degree structure but which are available also for personal enrichment. In contrast, the University of Keele is a much smaller and younger university offering an undergraduate degree of one prevailing pattern with a very wide range of choice within it; it takes four years for everyone (although there is soon to be a modification for a limited number permitting a three-year programme); it requires a first year of general education called a Foundation Year; two principal subjects are studied in the three years that follow with two subsidiary subjects for one year each; within these four subjects there has to be at least one science and one non-science for each undergraduate; the degree is offered at honours or pass standard depending on the level of performance and not on the content or length of the course. The higher degree and postgraduate arrangements are very similar to those at Birmingham on a narrower range of subjects in a smaller university and the same would be broadly true in music, art and drama. In addition, however, Birmingham has a metropolitan location, a range of residential accommodation for only a proportion of students, the rest living in lodgings or at home. Keele has a relatively rural location with campus accommodation for about 85 per cent of students. The life-styles for undergraduates are different and these two universities represent part of the pluralism of opportunity available between universities. Birmingham and Keele do quite different things at undergraduate level and they, like other universities, will need to be more explicit in future. The sense of belonging and participating is different in each, but the identity with a university, a place with a claim on intellectual excellence and a range of accommodation, equipment and staffing to match and back the quality, this identity in different ways they hold in common.

The bigger the universities get, the more they will have to attend to the features which enable students to feel that they belong to the institution and in the next decade this concern with belonging will have to contend with the very different view among some students and staff that the university is really a service station where fuel can be taken on board. In many large civic universities academic departments are, to change the metaphor, the main anchorage for students, together with halls of residence or colleges, and student societies and the Students' Union organization. These are the only purchase bringing a sense of identity a man or woman gets on the large organization, 'the University'.

The trends, for economic and 'efficiency' reasons, will be towards size in universities and binary institutions. Those which, like Keele, have identifiable academic programmes and university life-styles should preserve them while they offer a product which is, arguably, defensible. Those which, like Oxford or Cambridge or Exeter, have more varied academic programmes than Keele and university life-styles different but no less defensible, should seek to preserve these too. The large, civic and non-residential universities have life-styles which resemble those found in a metropolitan polytechnic. The standing and quality of the academic product of the university form a defence of its identity and must be preserved if quality is to survive. But it could apparently be easier for the binary and the university function to merge in Liverpool, in Manchester, in Newcastle than in Oxford or Cambridge or North Staffordshire where the organizational identities and the life-styles are noticeably different in the universities and the polytechnics and colleges concerned. I am, of course, leaving out of account the issues of modes of financing and government.

I expect to see pragmatic associations between universities and the binary system in the next decade or more. I believe there are too many administrative difficulties to make large-scale mergers likely and universities have too much variation between themselves to make a national plan feasible. In any case the sense of individual university pride and identity, at least among the academics, would render such a plan highly unlikely. Equally, the polytechnics have a pride and desire for identity of their own which would make them want to work at their own problems and devise their own plans, and at least some of them will seek recognition as universities in any case.

The situation could well be different with the colleges of education as they have had twenty-five years of association with universities through the Area Training Organizations. Even here, however, all experience suggests that the variety within the colleges is far too great to expect any systematic re-alignment with universities and all the prospects of what the James Committee will suggest make this even more remote. But some colleges want closer university associations and have resources to make this feasible, if only on a limited front to begin with.

Whatever national administrative and economic coherence might suggest, the history of the development of higher and further education is against quick mergers in the next decade, despite the spectacular growth in student numbers in both sectors. Universities vary, the UGC itself still has a unique function which ought not to be merged in some much larger Higher Education Commission. Polytechnics have yet to identify their systems of government and their relationship to the Department of Education and Science, and Local Education Authorities. Colleges of education have to discover their new identity after the decisions to be made on the James Report. Even though students seek to blur differences between the institutions, speaking of egalitarian principles and the coming multiversity, and even though the Open University builds bridges to a unit system of credits and the university of the air at home, the brute fact of a high quality, relatively brief undergraduate and postgraduate programme leads to a jealous concern for standards. This is a word too easily quoted by academics mounting high horses, but it is also a word indicating an ultimate intellectual austerity.

The multiple assumptions in thinking about the university of the future are all familiar, but are now coming together with a fresh urgency. 'Liberal values', the need for intellectual standards, undergraduate studies backed by a university concerned about research, professional studies relevant to society's needs whether in humanities, science or social science, manpower needs and the university-trained expert, the democratic right to higher education for those with ability, 'relevance' in university curricula, the student's right to study what he wants to, general and specific education, science and non-science in the undergraduate course, the university as a community, the government and a policy for higher education, accountability and efficiency—these are the pressing questions, and many of them apply to tertiary education as a whole. The next decade will show how far university values at their best can penetrate into all institutions of higher education and how far the unfounded superiorities of the universities can be displaced by the good qualities of the rest.

Notes

1 Data for this section of the essay have been obtained from the Department of Education and Science, from the Council for National Academic Awards, from the University of London, from the Association of Teachers in Colleges and Departments of Education and from a paper prepared by Dr James Topping,

formerly Vice-Chancellor of Brunel University, for a private conference of the Committee of Vice-Chancellors and Principals. I am glad to acknowledge these sources.

2 As for example by Sir John Wolfenden in the Stephenson Lecture for 1967 given at University College, London.

3 See *Student Relations*, HMSO, 25 July 1969, Vol. 1, pp. 57–9.

4 See *Third Report 1969–70*, *CPA*, HMSO, 24 July 1970.

5 E. Robinson: 'A Comprehensive Reform of Higher Education', *Higher Education Review*, Summer 1971, p. 15.

6 *Student Relations*, Vol. 1, p. 156.

7 As for example at Alsager College of Education in Cheshire.

Education for life

William Walsh

*Professor of Commonwealth Literature and Douglas Grant
Fellow at the University of Leeds*

In addressing myself to a subject so large that it can cause the writer to pant with the asthma of effort, so high that it induces him to puff at the ineffable, I shall try to keep in front of me the advice Donne gave as to the division of sermons into context, pretext and text. My remarks will be meant to glance, if even only out of the corner of the eye, first at the setting in which education takes place, secondly, at its purpose—given that has to do with 'life'—and thirdly, at the specification of the mind it aims to produce—given, also, that differences in the quality of life depend essentially on the kind of mind fostered by education.

I

In our society, in arts, sciences, or education, and particularly in higher education, there has been a marked growth in technical skill and professional competence. But clearly there is no necessary connection between this increase in means and the bringing about of the end they exist to serve: either an educated society or an educated individual. A good education persists, not as a collection of information, but as Coleridge pointed out,[1] as a certain unity of self, more or less coherent, more or less rich, and as a certain method of thinking and feeling, more or less complex, more or less sensitive. What lasts, what enters into us as a result of school and college, is a certain kind of charged awareness, a blend of value, attitude and assumption, a certain moral tone, a special quality of imagination, a particular flavour of sensibility—the things that give point and shape to our education. And it is in these that there has been in the modern world, together with the extension of technique, a severe contraction and enfeeblement, an impoverishment in those systems of tacit assumptions on which man has to base his character and conduct.

It is these 'beliefs' which flow into civilization and inform educational activity. They are the sources of good education when they are, to some degree, adequate to the complexity of the world they offer to interpret, when they are consonant with one another, and held with some degree of passion. They must combine sanity and sincerity. And it is here, at the source of action, where ultimate triumphs and disasters are prepared, that there has been in the modern world so notable a falling off in energy.

This state of affairs could not but reflect itself in the sensibility of our time and it is out of and through this sensibility that we live and learn. Sensibility I take here in the French sense as that special combination of thought, feeling, value and assumption, that particular flavour of taste and sentiment, that characteristic mode of action, which reveal the nuance and crystallize the tone and temper of a period. What first strikes an observer about our contemporary sensibility is the discrepancy between its overt behaviour and its inward condition. Outside we see toughness, realism, even ruthlessness; inside we see weakness, softness, an absence of any firmness and robustness of conviction: brutality without and vacancy within, a hard crust and a custard heart.

Next to conduct, nothing gives more intimate, more accurate testimony to the quality of feeling in a society and to its capacity for true relations than its use of language. It is hardly surprising, therefore, that so many have noted in our time a degeneration in language, a corruption in the essential means of thought and feeling. Language as it is used today exhibits a progressive dehumanization. We see this medium bleached of humanity in every sphere. We see it in the language of politics and administration, in the language of the social sciences and education: a Martian discourse, lethargic with passives and numb with the impersonal, emptied of contrasts, periphrastic, and as musical as the shutting of a filing cabinet—an image and a parable of the society language represents.

If this is the larger context—the life the students come from and return to—what about the narrower context of the university, at once so different and so like the society outside? There have been three phases in the development of the idea of the university in the recent past. There was the European concept, against which (in both senses) Robbins operated, which assumed—but only in a quiet, unemphatic way—that the university was an institution supported by the State for the benefit of the people, with an obligation to transform itself in tune with the changes occurring in society. But secondly it was assumed, as part of that idea, that the university was not simply an institution with a social reference and public duties. It was an idea. It was initiated by, it was organized around, it attempted to realize a conception. And if it was twisted away from some essential fidelity to its idea, then its centre was displaced and even the secondary effects of personal advancement, social service and national prestige would decay. If the idea was blurred, the expression would be mutilated.

The idea, of course, was of a society dedicated to the quest for and transmission of truth, which was not to be identified with the struggle for economic existence. Because truth was accessible to systematic enquiry, research was a fundamental concern of the university. And the scope of truth being more inclusive than that of any one discipline, the search for truth had to be guided by a vision of the one-ness of truth. Particular data were significant not for themselves but as one among many methods of getting at that one-ness. Unless related to the whole truth any one study became a meaningless and debilitating technique.

Because truth—or what at any moment is a provisional version of it—must also be transmitted, teaching is the other and equal concern of the university. University teaching brims over from research. Only those who strike the rock have the right to distribute the water. The relationship of teacher and taught in the university involves a Socratic equality of status and a common stress on standard, not on authority. University education was meant not for a handful of geniuses, not for the mediocre average, but for the minority capable of growth and initiative who yet stand in need of instruction.

The Robbins Report, composed when the universities were more and more encouraged to become—what?—instruments nervously registering degrees of change in the social temperature, set up a system of higher education in which the universities took on an immensely more comprehensive part than hitherto. Clearly there was implicit in the report a concept of the university, and clearly this concept sought to preserve most of the elements in the traditional idea. What was new was the redistribution of emphasis. Robbins put decidedly more stress on the role of the university as the supplier of social needs and required the university to be very much more conscious, very much more explicit, both about its social function and its pastoral office. Courses would have to be more pragmatically directed than they had habitually been, and the balance of faculties would have to be decided on explicitly social as well as academic grounds. Both these criteria, external and internal, had always operated, but one sensed that their order of importance had changed. In the modern world a third note was to be added to the research-teaching concept of the university, that of public service. The university was to break out of that decorative, private universe in which claret-coloured dons lolled among lotuses, into a more severely functional world, where immediate service to the community as well as that refracted kind it was accustomed to provide, was to be kept in the forefront of its concerns.

II

The pretext, the purpose of university activity, whichever one particular note in its theoretical constitution we wish to stress, has to do with the discovery and the communication of knowledge. That is its initiating concept and that is what flows through every form of its action in each period and every context. But there are two kinds of knowledge involved in any human activity, as Michael Oakeshott explains. On the one hand there is knowledge of technique which can be formulated into rules, deliberately learned, remembered and put into practice. On the other hand, there is the knowledge of practice, which cannot be formulated in rules; it is a tradition, a skill, an art—an art always whether the activity in question be poetic, scientific or religious. On the one side there is the cookery book; on the other, the art of cooking. On the one side, the Highway Code; on the other, the art of driving.

The distortion of modern life in thought, in living and learning comes from taking knowledge of technique to be the paradigm of all knowledge so that we prefer a blueprint to an educated skill, and an ideology to a habit of civilization. This is what in the modern world, preoccupied with certainty, abstraction and perfectibility, the sovereignty of reason has come to be. It means really the sovereignty of technique which is a gross abridgement of full, concrete human experience.[2] Modern thought—and scholarship and science—is the attempt to achieve an impossible perfection by bullying life into a copy of an already violently distorted rationalist cartoon.

If the general purpose of the university, and indeed of all kinds of higher education each in its own separate way, is the quest for and transmission of truth, its immediate purpose is so to order its management and teaching of the first kind of knowledge as to produce the second in the mind of the learner. By the communication of ideas it is to establish a style of thought. And that requires providing for students three kinds of experience, experience of the idea, experience of the imagination, and experience of intensity.

All our experience is embedded in variety, in that many-hued shading of fact which entails the act of choice, an act which in its turn depends—according to the idiom we select—upon essence or ideal or standard. This set of activities is put into action not simply by the variety of objects to be considered but by the variety of powers in the subject who considers them, as George Santayana pointed out:[3]

> For we have faculties, and habits, and impulses. These are
> the basis of our demands. And the demands, though variable,
> constitute an ever-present intrinsic standard of value by which
> we feel and judge. The ideal is immanent in them; for the
> ideal means the fulfilment in which our faculties would find
> their first employment and their most congenial world.
> Perfection would be nothing but life under those conditions.
> Accordingly our consciousness of the ideal becomes distinct
> in proportion to the vigour and definiteness with which our
> faculties work.

A concern with the ideal is certainly a function of maturity. But it does not begin then. It is part—vaguely and imperceptibly, it is true—of our earliest human responses and it enters into our primary, even our primitive, perceptions. The appreciation of difference carries with it the possibility of preference and the whole moral world. We cannot, therefore, limit the term reality to immediate and palpable aspects of existence since it is the ideal aspect that endows it with character and human worth.

Human nature exists as part of ordinary nature. But the character of developed or educated human nature is above all to work with reference to an ideal which is consonant with its instincts and reflected in its thought and action. The business of educated nature, in fact, is to live what Santayana calls 'the life of reason'. And the business of the life of reason (and of education which should be a practical apprenticeship to it) and above all of a higher education directed to making an effect upon living, is to make its ideal at once more human and more relevant to the complexity of reality. Its worth is to be gauged by its success in turning the uneducated mind with a crude ideal into the articulate one with a refined and appropriate ideal.

Coleridge, in one of his homelier anecdotes, describes the mind

K

as a garden covered with weeds, and the business of education as being 'to prejudice the soil towards roses and strawberries'.[4] In fostering that 'prejudice towards roses', a bias in favour of the ideal, upon which depends the humanity of the individual and the quality of civilization, the strongest appeal should be to the imagination, the power by which the student prises himself free from the present and loosens the clutch of the immediate. In the imaginative act the student disengages himself from the partial and the broken, 'from the universe as a mass of little parts', and comes to conceive of a larger unity and the more inclusive whole. The realm of now and here is immensely extended and complicated:[5]

> . . . impulse and power should be given to the intellect, and the ends of a moral being be exhibited. For this object thus much is effected by works of imagination; that they carry the mind out of self, and show the possible of the good and the great in the human character. . . . In the imagination of man exists the seeds of all moral and scientific improvement; chemistry was first alchemy, and out of astrology sprang astronomy. In the childhood of those sciences the imagination opened a way, and furnished materials, on which the ratiocinative powers in a maturer stage operated with success. The imagination is the distinguishing characteristic of man as a progressive being; and I repeat that it ought to be carefully guided and strengthened as the indispensable means and instrument of continued amelioration and refinement.

Imagination, it will be seen, receives an importance as an educative agency greater than the attenuated respect given it by most modern educators. For these to exercise the imagination is to cultivate a sense of the aesthetic. And this, in a civilization which confounds the artist with the aesthete, and confuses the severity and the chastity of the one with the preciousness and frivolity of the other, means a trivial and decorative addition to more seriously important human powers. But imagination is not a garnish of the soul, a mere finish according to a fashionable specific. 'The rules of the imagination are themselves the very powers of growth and production.'[6] The life of the young is quick with the propulsive energies of imagination which 'carry

the mind out of self'; the duty of education is to bring before
the learner works of imagination of such quality (and science is
also a human achievement imaginatively initiated) that 'they show
the possible of the good and great in the human character'. The
bleakness and the dehumanizing influence of so much education
comes from confining imagination to a cramped parish of aesthetic
activity. But imagination is the air in which new knowledge
breathes, as it is the salt preserving the savour of the old.
'Knowledge', it has been said, 'does not keep any better than fish.'

Imagination is not only the core of experience, part of perception
itself; it is also the means by which experience is shared. Without
it we should stay gaoled in our private darkness. With it we enter
into different lives, discover other minds and enjoy what they
discover. To share with another is to be joined to him, and
imagination is the great unifier of humanity:[7]

> . . . men's perceptions may be various, their powers of
> understanding very unequal, but the imagination is, as it
> were, the self-consciousness of instinct, the contribution
> which the inner capacity, and demand of mind make to
> experience.

Imagination melts the boundaries of sharply separated lives and
breaks down the cells of excessive individuality in the interests of
a more inclusive reality. A man can say, Santayana wrote in the
same place, 'I have imagination and nothing that is real is alien
to me'.

Experiences of the ideal, experiences of imagination, but also
experiences of intensity. Clearly a function of education is the
expansion of the consciousness, the extension of awareness, by
learning. But the knowledge in any mind, however moderate, is
never a mere aggregation of components. It composes a structure.
Keats was one who realized that no matter how expansive a
knowledge and how exceptional the mind, its knowledge is
organized under only one or two fundamental themes or interests:
'the two uppermost thoughts in a man's mind are the two poles
of his world, he revolves on them and everything is southward
and northward to him through their means. We take but three
steps from feathers to iron.'[8]

Part, one of the most important parts surely, of the life of a
student in higher education, is to discover the two poles of his

K*

world and to learn to take the three steps from feathers to iron. Or, from the teacher's viewpoint, one has above all in education, as Henry James put it, to discover and stir the 'subjective passion'. On these experiences—and they may be few—when they are crucial and alive, hang all our systematic opinions, and the enduring value of the latter depends on the degree in which they keep the former present and active. It is in particular experiences, marked by intensity and concentration, when emotion is powerful and distinct, that taste and value are formed. As George Santayana said:[9]

> ... preferences then grown conscious, judgments then put
> into words, will reverberate through calmer hours; they will
> constitute prejudices, habits of apperception, secret standards
> for all other beauties. A period of life in which such
> intuitions have been frequent may amass tastes and ideals
> sufficient for the rest of our days. . . . Half our standards
> come from our first masters, and the other half from our
> first loves.

III

So much for context and pretext. What of the text? That will be no more than a hint or suggestion about the quality of the mind which has been, in a serious sense, prepared for life. But I should make my point more sharply if I said a suggestion about the mind which has prepared itself for life in the context of the university. Like knowledge itself, education is fundamentally self-created, and however important the occasion, or the context, success ultimately depends upon the capacity of the mind to initiate its own progress. In this sense the function of higher education, and supremely that of the university, is to provide a context, sympathetic and provoking, in which self-education can take place. We all begin with our original endowment, our shared human capacity, but no-one graduates into adulthood, least of all intellectual adulthood, by the simple progress of an original endowment. One has—in this context, the student has—to make a fundamental choice. He has, without the least haze of portentousness, to elect for seriousness. He has to decide against the volatility of impulse and in favour of the life of reason. It is a decision which cannot, in fact, be avoided. Those who think it can have simply opted for the other side. This decision is the spring of that set of dispositions and qualities marking the mature mind, the mind, I began by saying, distinguished by unity of self and method in thinking and feeling.

The first of the qualities is the disinterestedness gained from recognizing that an order does exist which cannot be compromised by expediency or sacrificed to anything itself—the order which is implicit in the integrity of science or the discipline of scholarship. Secondly, such a mind, because of a comparatively extensive range of knowledge, shows itself alert to fact and the possessor of a tonic sense of reality. That is a quality which requires from its cultivator effort and energy. Keats, whose extraordinary transformation from Cockney to classic in so short a space was a brilliant and exemplary exercise in self-education, thoroughly understood this fact, when he wrote 'every mental pursuit takes its reality and worth from the ardour of the pursuer'. But this activity has to be accompanied, as Keats also saw, by 'the absence of any irritable reaching after fact and reason', the capacity to be still and receptive without any 'buzzing here and there without any knowledge of what is to be arrived at'. Nothing, he said, 'is finer for the purpose of great productions than a very gradual ripening of the intellectual powers'. And this ability to attend calmly and not to force is the intellectual equivalent of the virtue of rational humility, itself an expression above all of the sense of reality.

Education is only the most economic, the least wasteful and most effective form of organized general human development. The supremely important part of that development which education, and above all higher education, has to pursue is, in its own context, and with instruments appropriate to its own nature, 'to school an intelligence and make it a soul'.[10] Some may think this Keatsian formulation a trifle overblown, though in my view raising a gleam of spirituality in a world of Philistinism is indeed a proper function of higher education, and particularly if there is any justice in the character I gave earlier to the context in which we live. Perhaps one ought to put the essential point more soberly. Perhaps one should say more drably and more modestly that higher education will make a difference to the quality of living to the degree in which it can prepare minds capable of bringing to bear upon the complexities of existence a standard at once cogent and humane. Or that what we want from the university is an education that promotes a finer quality of life because it alters the nature of the living mind.

Notes

1   *The Friend*, II, 4.
2   Cf. *Rationalism in Politics*, M. Oakeshott, London, 1962, pp. 117–20.
3   *The Sense of Beauty*, London, 1896, pp. 260-2
4   *Table Talk*, 21 July 1830.
5   *Lectures on Shakespeare*, XI.
6   *Biographia Literaria*, XVIII.
7   *Interpretation of Poetry and Religion*, G. Santayana, London, 1900, p. 9.
8   *The Letters of John Keats*, Maurice Buxton Forman, ed., London, 1947, p. 112.
9   *The Life of Reason*, Vol. IV, London, 1905, p. 194.
10 *Letters*, p. 337.

Appendix

The use and interpretation of student–staff ratios[1]

F. J. Orton

Academic Secretary, University of Sheffield

Methods of calculating student/academic staff ratios, their main uses, and guides to interpretation provided for the committees concerned, are of intense contemporary interest. Experience in the use of these figures and guides has indicated some dangers and limitations which are worth discussion.

Information provided

Eight statistical tables are provided annually in the University of Sheffield. For each Department these indicate:

a   Undergraduate and postgraduate full-time student equivalents,
b   Weighted and unweighted total student equivalents,[2]
c   Full-time and part-time staff on University funds,[3]
d   £ spent on part-time demonstrators,
e   £ department grant,
f   Weighted and unweighted student/academic staff ratios,
g   Weighted and unweighted student/technical staff ratios,
h   Academic staff/clerical staff ratios.

These are based as far as possible on the academic weight placed on the various subjects that each individual student is taking in the year in question. For example, a first-year student studying three equal subjects is attributed in student equivalent terms in equal proportions (i.e. one-third each) to the three departments involved; or a third-year student, sitting ten papers of equal importance, the teaching for one of which is provided by Department B while the rest of the course is covered by Department A, will be attributed 0·9 student equivalents to Department A and 0·1 student equivalents to Department B. This system operates over nearly two-thirds of the total University student population but in areas with closely integrated courses, e.g. in the applied sciences, an analysis of students' timetables is necessary to provide the basis of the division into student equivalents. This division will depend on the number of hours of instruction (lectures, laboratory classes, tutorials, etc.) which a student receives from each department. This information is obtained from an analysis of the timetables of the students concerned. Of the two systems used, the former is preferable since the figures are then based on broad academic decisions. The method has one invariable rule: the total number of unweighted student equivalents must equal the total number of full-time students plus the allowance which is given for the load represented by part-time students. Part-time postgraduates *registered* for higher degrees count as 0·75 and departments are also given an allowance for post-graduate short-courses, depending on the length of the course and the number of students: part-time undergraduate and occasional students are also included on the basis of the length and content of the course. Students who are not in the University for one term during the session, e.g. language students studying abroad for one term, are counted as 0·80. This gives the department some allowance for their supervisory work during the period abroad.

For clinical medicine and clinical dentistry overall figures of staff and students are provided since a breakdown of student load by departments has proved impracticable.

Relationships between figures

With some exceptions the larger the department the less favourable the student-staff ratio (the term 'favourable' is applied to those departments with the lower student-staff ratio). This gives expression to the view that it takes no more staff time to lecture to a large class than it does to a small one though it makes the assumption that the larger departments are usually lecturing to the larger classes. There does, therefore, seem to be evidence of economy of scale between different-sized departments in the University.

The significance of the relationship existing between the size of the department (measured by the number of full-time staff equivalents plus the staff equivalents of part-time demonstrators)[4] and the mean of the weighted and unweighted student-academic staff ratio, can be illustrated by the equation:

$$\frac{s}{t} = at^{0.5} + b \qquad \qquad \text{Equation I}$$

when t = number of academic staff equivalents and s = student equivalents (for 1970-1 $a = 1.18$ and $b = 5.55$). The relationship was significant at the five per cent level in that year while in some previous years it has been significant at the one per cent level.

A regression analysis of the type $t = f(s)$ will almost certainly be significant at the one per cent probability level in any University but Equation I can be adapted to the form:

$$s = at^{1.5} + bt \qquad \qquad \text{Equation II}$$

The student/staff ratio taken for the equation is the mean of the weighted student/staff ratio and the unweighted ratio, but one further adjustment is made to overcome one of the main anomalies in the UGC weighting system. Students in the fourth and fifth years of four- or five-year courses are weighted as postgraduates.

While the calculations assume that economies of scale can always be achieved, however large the department, in practice of course a stage is reached where duplication of classes may be necessary and there is therefore an upper limit of size above which the equation is inapplicable. Furthermore, the equation is probably inadequate to represent a department with fewer than three members of the academic staff. The values of t, therefore, for which these equations are applicable are limited but where these limits lie is subject to discussion and further investigation.

While Equation I reflects the proportionate difference between departments, it is also possible to calculate from Equation II the theoretical *number* of staff for any given number of student equivalents and therefore the theoretical number of staff by which any department is in surplus or deficit compared with the mean.

The significance of the equation combined with the fundamental reasoning of the first paragraph of this section suggests that over the range of departmental size in the University of Sheffield economies of scale can be expected to operate in respect of the number of academic staff required to teach increasing numbers of students. Nevertheless it can be argued that the particular significance shown might be the result of the inferior bargaining position of a large department. For a small department with a few members of staff to argue that they cannot between them cover a particular option is a plausible and much used technique in the battle for resources. A large department using the same tactic will usually fail, yet the actual position may be no different in a rapidly developing subject.

Variations

By using Equation I it is possible to predict the average student/ staff ratio that 'should' pertain for a department of a given size. This varies from a mean ratio of the order of eight students per member of staff for a small department with four staff, to a ratio of the order of twelve students per member of staff for a large department with thirty-six staff.

The interesting figure is the variation between the actual student/staff ratio and the ratio predicted on the basis of the size of a particular department. This difference gives an indication of variations between departments in their ratios which cannot be explained by the size of the department and is a reasonable first indicator of the order of need for extra (or less) staff. This order is shown annually in a Table of Unfavourability.

Uses

The equation relating academic staff and students is used for three main purposes:

a   to provide a yardstick based on a purely mathematical technique for the use of resource-allocating committees considering requests for extra staff, department by department.

b   to provide the data to set in motion a review procedure of the establishment of those departments that are very favourably situated. In the case of these departments, if a vacancy occurs, a Faculty Board has to present a strong case for retention of the post in that department. The departments concerned have not had replaced three out of the five posts reviewed and the money made available has been used to foster new developments.

c to provide one of the criteria for requesting additional academic posts in the quinquennial plan for 1972–7.

The basic figures of student equivalents are used by a large number of committees, not only those allocating recurrent funds but also those concerned with the provision of teaching accommodation and library space. The committees concerned, however, use the figures and the 'Table of Unfavourability' with very considerable discretion, as guides to and not as substitutes for reasoning; nevertheless, it has become accepted that departments in the 'most favourable' quarter of the table are likely to have difficulty in obtaining additional academic staff posts while those in the least favourable quarter stand some chance.

Scepticism

The system and its application has been accepted in the University though with a degree of healthy scepticism which, it is to be hoped, will continue. This acceptance rests not least on the belief that it is preferable to argue from figures than to rest the case for a particular post on the advocacy of a particular member of a Committee. Each department is sent, with requests for comment, a copy of the working sheet used for the calculation of its total student equivalents and heads of departments know they have been consulted at an early stage. Equations I and II have probably been accepted through a desire for simplicity, for the 'Table of Unfavourability' is used to compress a complex of different statistics into one admittedly over-simplified list. On the other hand the statistical basis of the equation has interested a number of my academic colleagues who have made suggestions about its compilation and use. The particular visual presentation used when the Table was first presented also caught the imagination of the committees concerned. There are enough departments in the University with a wide spread of size to make the calculation of the equation possible; the number of large departments has grown during this quinquennium and has helped provide a good spread of different sizes from three to thirty-eight staff per department.

The theoretical danger of the approach is that once accepted it could be used with little recognition of the approximations and the assumptions of the statistical techniques used. While some may argue that their department is above the 'Orton line' (the popular name for the equation) by three posts and therefore, they contend, this proves beyond doubt that the department must have this extra staff, the committees concerned have had ample experience of the technique and are fully aware of the nature of the figures presented. Committees have always used the material as a guide only. The personalization (the 'Orton line') of what is intended to be an impersonal statistical approach may be regretted by the author but it may accidentally have helped in its acceptance. A possible job description of the University administrator is 'honest broker' and the academic body probably recognizes that the particular statistical approach adopted is coloured by that definition of a Registrar's Office.

The healthy scepticism of my academic colleagues is based on a number of important points. All the figures (except those of staff establishment) are approximations. The input/output ratios of staff to students take account of the University commitment to teach only and (apart from postgraduate output) no account is taken of the commitment to research. Since research falls as a duty equally on all members of the academic staff, the lack of a measure of research output is not an over-whelming criticism if the figures are used for internal university purposes only.

The figures present a statistical argument for or against extra posts for the current year. Any posts thus created will be provided for the following year. Logically, therefore, the committees concerned should judge staff requirements on the scale of next session's teaching load but this is rarely possible to forecast. (A major change such as the 50 per cent expansion in medicine, together with the 20 per cent expansion in dentistry, planned to start in October 1971, was covered by a special analysis of the effect of this expansion on student/staff ratios.) When resources are in short supply most departments have to obtain the students first and argue for additional staff later.

No account is taken of the number of staff contact hours taken to teach any particular group of students. It can be argued that this number of contact hours is a function itself of the favourable staff position of the department concerned and a system of resource allocation based on contact hours encourages over-teaching and the proliferation of options. Some of my academic colleagues disagree with this argument strongly.

The provision of both weighted and unweighted student equivalents provides a duality of information which individuals use to their own advantage, selecting the particular statistic which will bolster their arguments. While this enables confusion to be sown, the provision of two figures can be defended on the basis that it emphasizes the existence of an area of uncertainty in all the statistics used. Some more carefully calculated measure of this area might, however, serve this latter purpose better. The information shortly to be available from the Committee of Vice-Chancellors and Principals on the use of staff time might produce data on which a more appropriate weighting for postgraduates can be based.

Other comparisons

The application of this statistical method has demonstrated variations in student/staff ratios not only between different individual departments but also between different areas of the University. The variations may be due to perfectly valid reasons such as special academic needs or the particular development of the subject in the University at the present time; for instance, it is generally accepted that clinical medicine must continue to rely on small group teaching since no other method would be possible (the advent of colour television in educational technology as applied to medicine may marginally affect the argument). On the other hand, the variation between groups of subjects or departments may be the result of more favourable treatment in the past and which in changed circumstances is no longer justified. Inter-University international comparisons might help in providing further guides, but such exercises are full of pitfalls. Undertaken with care the comparison of standardized data about broad subject groups in universities in the United Kingdom is a feasible task, but techniques of valid international comparison are more difficult to develop and in the present state of knowledge may mislead. The direct comparison of the student/staff ratio for the same faculty in two universities will give very little, if any, helpful information. It is much more valuable to compare the degree to which the student/staff ratio in Faculty A of University B varies from the mean student/staff ratio of that University as against the extent to which the student/staff ratio in Faculty X of University Y varies from the mean student/staff ratio of that University. Even when these comparisons are made, the subjects covered by the two Universities B and Y must be similar, as must the departments of the two Faculties A and X.

Yardsticks of the type illustrated in this paper can never be more than helpful guides; but the danger that the technique may itself be a constraint on the imaginative development of the University can be averted as long as the methods used and the basic principles behind them are kept continually under review.

Notes

1 While the observations in this document are entirely those of the author, this paper gives me the opportunity to thank my academic and administrative colleagues in the University for their help and encouragement in this work.

2 The weighted figures are founded on the University Grants Committee's system of weighting: 1 for undergraduates and for postgraduate students reading for the Diploma in Education; 2 for all other postgraduate students in arts-based subjects and 3 for all postgraduates in science-based subjects.

3 Staff numbers include those paid from general University funds only. Staff equivalents are calculated by counting those members of the academic staff on salary ranges lower than the career grade of lecturer (i.e. experimental officers, research assistants, lecteurs and the like) as one half of a full-time member of the academic staff.

4 This is based on the assumption that the £2,000 spent on part-time demonstrators could equally have been spent on establishing one extra academic staff post at lecturer level.

Index